Gary Morland is a gifted communicator lessons the hard way. He grew up in a dysfunctional family and went down that road himself, bottoming out as a confused alcoholic with a wife, two daughters, and no idea how to change. God transformed Gary's life through his grace and the practical advice of wise mentors. Those lessons are passed along in this powerful and insightful book.

John Fuller, cohost of *Focus on the Family*

We have all sat through a million sermons about grace, read books and sung songs about grace, yet many of us live our lives as if we've never heard the word. *A Family Shaped by Grace* is a powerful testimony of God's goodness and grace. Gary gives incredible insight into the supernatural peacefulness God has available for every family. His practical guidance will give you the tools you need to lead your family into peace with both confidence and excellence.

Jimmy Myers, PhD, LPC-S, author of *Fearless Parenting: Raising a Faithful Child in a Secular Culture*

I'm thankful for a voice like Gary Morland speaking into our generation about family and grace and how God can make all things new. This book is an excellent read and will be an inspiration to many.

Annie F. Downs, bestselling author of *Looking for Lovely* and *Let's All Be Brave*

There are elders who speak with the authority of hard-won wisdom. Gary Morland is just such an elder. In *A Family Shaped by Grace*, Morland shares tools for crafting the kind of family we all want with family members who love well, serve well, and work together toward something eternal. Pick up a copy, and learn the art of family-craft from your elder; you'll find Morland's experience colors him with the patina of something very trustworthy.

Seth Haines, author of *Coming Clean: A Story of Faith*

A FAMILY
SHAPED
by
GRACE

A FAMILY SHAPED — by — GRACE

How to Get Along with the People Who Matter Most

GARY MORLAND

Ʀ
Revell

a division of Baker Publishing Group
Grand Rapids, Michigan

© 2017 by Gary Morland

Published by Revell
a division of Baker Publishing Group
P.O. Box 6287, Grand Rapids, MI 49516-6287
www.revellbooks.com

Printed in the United States of America

Library of Congress Cataloging-in-Publication Data is on file at the Library of Congress, Washington, DC.

ISBN 978-0-8007-2795-6

Published in association with the literary agency of The Fedd Agency, Inc., P.O. Box 341973, Austin, TX 78734.

17 18 19 20 21 22 23   7 6 5 4 3 2 1

Brenda—I wish it hadn't taken so long to realize
how easy and sweet it is to love you.

Myquillyn and Emily—Every single day of my
life is better because God made you daughters
to me and sisters to each other.

Chad and John—I wish every dad with daughters could
have the peace I get from you being husbands to mine.

Tracy—Remember that time I beat you in ping-pong, left-
handed, while holding a kid? I know sometimes you forget.

Alyson—"I love you and I'm glad you're my sister." Yes, visit.

Harold—Every day your voice comes out of me.

Family is a verb. Family is not just what we are, it's something that we keep on actively making.

Ann Voskamp

Contents

Foreword

We always knew Dad had a book in him; we just figured one of us would have to write it for him. We weren't sure he would be able to consolidate all his notes in one place. Dad has been taking notes on God and life and family for the past twenty-eight years, filling up stacks of lined yellow legal pads and four-by-six index cards, then his iPhone notes app, now this book. This is a bigger deal than you can possibly know for two reasons.

First, Dad never learned to type with his fingers in the correct typing position, so this whole manuscript was pecked out with two index fingers and a whole lot of heart.

Second, Dad wasn't a believer for most of our childhood. He didn't even go to church for show or out of duty. Instead, he stayed home every Sunday morning, drank beer, and listened to Bruce Springsteen records. We still remember the morning he reenacted the concert version of *Born in the USA* for us in the living room, a rare Sunday when Mom went to church without us girls. He dimmed the lights, cranked the stereo, and lip-synched the whole thing, complete with white T-shirt and red hat in his back pocket.

But life with Dad when we were little wasn't always so light-hearted. Most of our childhood memories involve an alcoholic father who was there but not fully present, alive but not fully awake. Until one day Dad stopped drinking, and awhile after that, he told us he accepted Jesus. That's when the story gets interesting.

This book is about what happened next, about how a man who never had a proper role model of a healthy family life learned to be a husband and father so that we could never say we didn't have a proper role model of a healthy family life.

As his daughters, we have had a front-row seat to the difference God makes in the life of a person. We finally got to see the man Dad was always meant to be.

This unlikely story of grace and forgiveness will help cast a hopeful vision for you if you're desperate for some accessible encouragement and practical advice. Dad's gentle instruction will be a kind companion for you in the midst of your own difficult family relationships.

It's a rare kind of gift when your dad writes a book because you get to see him as a person and not just a dad. He talks about Mom as his best friend, but not the kind of friends who get airbrushed T-shirts made with each other's faces on them. It's the kind of friendship that when he says something semi-dumb and Mom rolls her eyes at him, he laughs instead of getting defensive. Meanwhile all the grandkids are watching how they act and are taking notes on how to be an adult.

Dad is a man who is often out of the loop when we get together with Mom because he can't keep up with all our talking and laughing, but he loves to be in the room anyway.

He's a Poppy who co-plans Grandy Camp with Mom every summer for all six of their grandkids, complete with opening and closing ceremonies.

He's an introvert who loves people and a chronic encourager who always chooses hope, even in the darkness.

Most of all, Dad is a believer who knows his sufficiency rests in the person of Jesus Christ, and his life reflects that truth.

He loves well, with lots of grace and curiosity, and his philosophy of family is both simple and oddly profound. We're proof—we all truly like each other and when we fight, we always make up.

So that's who you're settling down with as you read this book. Our dad, a man we've known and loved and laughed with (and at) all of our lives. You're going to love him too. We're giddy that we get to share him with you.

Myquillyn and Emily, Gary and Brenda's girls

P.S. In this book you'll meet a man named Harold. We remember him as a wise friend of Dad's who had a gentle disposition and always wore a green sport coat. We always knew Harold helped shape our family's dynamics as Dad's mentor, and we feel as if we should set aside one special day a year to wear green jackets in his honor. Thank you, Harold.

P.P.S. If you wish you had a Harold in your own life but don't, we're quite sure Dad can fill in for Harold for you in this book. Green jacket optional.

Yes, You Can Get There from Here

You and I are at Panera. I get the Pick 2 with a Frontega Chicken Panini, tomato soup, and chips, and you get the broccoli cheddar soup in a bread bowl. I take a bite, and you start sharing about your family, your family relationships, and how you feel.

You talk about how much you love them and how it's so natural to sacrifice and work hard for them. You describe how you try to create a supportive, loving atmosphere. You try to put their needs before yours. You love them, and you just want everybody to get along and to root for each other.

But no matter how much you do or how much you sacrifice, you're frustrated with some important pieces of your family relationships.

No matter how good some pieces are, some other pieces always drag things down. Sometimes you sense a growing wall in your marriage, but other times you think it's great. You're pretty sure you feel a cold distance every time you're around the in-laws, "but maybe it's just me?" Then whenever you're feeling good about your marriage and in-laws, the older kids act like they hate each other and it's breaking your heart.

It's Always Something

Maybe things are great as long as your family is just you guys in the house, but whenever a holiday or vacation comes, you get sick to your stomach knowing the tension and misunderstandings that are present in the rest of the family, or in that one particular you-know-who.

Maybe you and the grown kids continually butt heads about how they live and the decisions they make. Maybe you're the grown kid, and you long to live and make your own decisions without offending your parents.

You're frustrated with how some members of your family relate to each other, and you're frustrated with how some of those relationships relate to you. The tension between your estranged brother and sister is really none of your business, is it? But because you love them, it hurts you when they're so hateful to each other.

You hardly talk about it, and you hate to admit it, but sometimes you feel misunderstood, underappreciated, and even rejected by some. You'll never bring that up though, because it's not about you.

Then there's that one relationship. You've about given up on it. Hopelessness is depressing, so you're not going to talk about that one either. Just move on.

Overall, you want everyone to get along. You know they want to get along, and you know it would be best for everyone. But you don't know how to make it happen. You've been doing everything you can, and it's not enough.

Your soup's getting cold.

You've always felt that changing a few things might make a big difference, but you haven't known exactly which things or how to do it. You've even been willing to take it all on yourself and change your attitude and expectations—if only you knew the attitude and expectations that would help.

You're telling yourself that things are going OK, and they are, but you really wish some of these relational holes could get filled in. And you're afraid some of those holes might be getting deeper.

You pause. You scan my face for signs of discouragement or even shock. You kick yourself a little inside for saying so much.

It's Always Way Better Than It Looks

I smile and you think maybe I'm laughing at you, then you realize the whole time you were holding your spoon halfway between your mouth and your bread bowl, never taking a bite. Now it's your turn to eat, and I start talking.

"Your family can become more and more a source of satisfaction and fulfillment and less and less a source of disappointment and discouragement."

Your shoulders relax a bit.

"You can make a difference in how your family members treat each other, and you can feel better about how they treat you. You can appreciate your family for who they are now and for who you know they can be, and you can contribute to a growing closeness."

Your soup seems to have warmed up. I lean forward a bit to make sure you hear this.

"Your marriage *can* be better. Your relationships with your parents and siblings can be better. That parents–grown kids thing can be better and so can that mother-in-law–daughter-in-law thing. And not only better, it can be satisfying, even joyful.

"And that one challenging relationship you can't even acknowledge? It's not hopeless. I promise.

"You can know what to expect from your family and exactly how to help everyone get closer. You can even become the wise family version of a Jedi Master, knowing what to accept and what to try to change, respected for being an example of the things that deep down they all know are best."

You never really got that Star Wars stuff, but the idea of being a master in your family sounds good.

"You'll pay a price, but Jedi Masters always do. It will be worth it, because years from now you will rest in the peace that you have deeply affected your family legacy.

"You'll look back and know you didn't just survive, you didn't just provide nurture and direction; you deeply influenced the people God created them to be. And in doing that, you influenced all the people they influence, now and later. You will have dented the world with grace. All because of your family.

"You'll feel better, even about the one you can't talk about."

You feel your heart smiling. "Really? So how can this happen?" you say. "How can we get there?"

The rest of the conversation is in this book. This is when you begin wooing their hearts, one drop of grace at a time.

Here's Where Our Conversation Leads

First, I'll share my family's own story of going way down and going way up, so you can picture the kind of change that can happen in your family. You may need more change than we did, or you may need just a piece of the kind of change we've made. Whatever you need, you'll see how rediscovering some lost tools makes change simple and possible.

In the remainder of part 1, you'll start to see your family as perhaps you've never seen them before. You'll take a Family Satisfaction Assessment to reveal how you really feel about them and about your most challenging relationships. You'll learn how wonderful your family experience can be, and you'll discover the big obstacles, the *Everyday Tactics of Family Disharmony*, that are keeping you from it.

In part 2, I'll introduce the *Timeless Tools of Family Peace*—and then they won't be lost to you anymore! You'll see how they can all work together to create a wonderful momentum in your family. You'll find that your family is already wired for that contagious momentum to take hold. You'll be encouraged to learn this is not a burden of work for you but a simple progressive exchanging of old attitudes and actions for new ones that will make your relationships easier and more fulfilling.

In part 3, you'll find practical suggestions for what the *Timeless Tools* could look like in your family. And I'll give you a plan you can adapt to take one big step in your most challenging family relationship.

By the end of this book, your heart, soul, and mind will be inspired and prepared to see grace and acceptance replace performance and manipulation, even in your most challenging family relationships.

Back at Panera the café clerk has picked up our plates, but our conversation is just getting started. Can I get you a cup of coffee or tea?

Part 1

YOUR RIVER

We must begin thinking like a river if we are to leave
a legacy of beauty and life for future generations.

David Brower

1

My Wife's Husband

If Our River Can Change, So Can Yours

Failure is only failure if it happens in the last chapter. Otherwise it's a plot point. People put the book down too soon.

Danny Iny

In 1985, my wife's husband is thirty-four years old and an alcoholic who drinks three quarts of beer a day and falls asleep on the floor every night by 7:00 p.m.

He's a college dropout with no training or skills, no ambition, and no motivation. He's lost, apart from God, unemployed half the time, and drives an old Chevy Vega with a driver's side door that flies open every time he makes a right turn. He drinks behind her back and lies about it, and she learns she can't trust him.

My wife lives with this man in a nine-hundred-square-foot house with lots of arguing, mostly because he's clueless about how to be a good husband or raise kids. He vows to himself not to have children until he "figures out how to be an adult," but he never does and here they are, two daughters eleven and eight.

That's my wife's life. This is normal for a long time.

I'm the husband.

That's how our family starts and how it goes for the first twelve years of our marriage. No one has any reason to believe anything will ever change.

It changes.

Not overnight but over time. Today our marriage centers on grace and patience and caring more for the other person than for ourselves. Most of our arguments are over giving the other person their way (yes, we argue over sacrificing for each other). We're best friends. Trust dominates and creates an inviting vibe in our home. Disagreements are brief and hardly an inch deep.

We share a rich connection as a family with our daughters, their husbands, and their kids, and people seem to notice.

How does this change happen?

It should have come from the family in which I grew up, but it didn't. Mine was a nice middle-class family but purposeless, with its own unique dysfunctions. Dad was an alcoholic, and his unstable presence dominated our family mood. We all knew the rules: Thou shalt not upset Dad. Avoid anything controversial or confrontational. His inner anger broke out almost daily at home in loud, yelling monologues aimed at no one but intended for everyone to hear. Rants began for no reason; Dad upset with the world. Often I'd hear him yelling from downstairs, "Does anybody hear me!" as if he wanted someone to argue with, to vent to, but everyone was upstairs trying to avoid him.

We walked on tiptoes when he quieted down, hoping he'd go to sleep. Later, he reminded me of that guy in the Bible who lived in the tombs, shouting and hurting himself and no one dared go near him.

Ours was the classic stereotype of the addicted family where everyone is an enabler because it's too painful to confront.

Like on our spring break trip to Florida. Dad and I are going to check out colleges. Mom's at work. I'm packed and ready, and the old Impala pulls in the driveway and just sits there. I wait, then go outside. The car is running, and Dad's slumped over the wheel. I know Mom's not going to like it if Dad blows our trip, so I scoot him into the passenger seat, load the bags, and start driving south. Two hours later in Kentucky, he slowly wakes up, chin on his chest, opening one eye at me, realizing what's happened.

"You're a good boy," he says groggily. And I'm just relieved he's not mad. I've learned my job is to do whatever it takes to maintain peace and not deal with anything. To me, this is normal.

But there's a problem: *I don't know what normal is.* I never learn what healthy family relationships look like. I just react in whatever way will hold down turmoil and help me survive. Defensiveness becomes normal. Being offended is normal. Arguing is normal. Reacting out of my emotions is normal. Doing something purposeful with or for my family? Seeing "grace" in my family? What's that? That's not normal.

Your Normal Is Normal to You

Maybe in your immediate or extended family, you have learned over the years that patterns and behaviors repeat themselves in family relationships. You watch as average problems are treated like crises. And the crises come to be accepted as unavoidable. You see some family members so worried about themselves that they have no room for understanding or generosity. Others seem to major on how they're treated, how they're wronged and offended, or how they're misunderstood and underappreciated.

Some members of your family seem to collect offenses and misunderstandings as if it's a contest. Others are afraid to live their own lives because someone else might be offended. Still others seem eager to give offense, to try to give back what they think has been given to them. Sometimes it seems as if each person is convinced they understand everyone else, but no one else understands them, and each one is working very hard to convince the others of their lack of understanding.

Sometimes much of this is rolled into one person, and sometimes that person becomes your nemesis.

Usually, everyone doesn't do all these things. And some don't do any. But many do some, which often leads to an emotional disconnection and even physical avoidance of each other, sometimes for years. No one really knows how to restore the relationship. Everyone waits for someone else to take the initiative.

You reject many of these patterns and behaviors. You know better. But you don't reject all of them. You don't reject all of them because some of them seem normal to you. Those are the ones you keep and pass on. Just a few. Which is what everyone you have observed in your family has done, each one passing on just a few dysfunctions, which adds up to all of them showing up in your entire family.

You grow up thinking you're stuck with how family relationships turn out. You assume relationships are not something you have much influence over. Instead, you react to disagreements and offenses without any guiding purpose, assuming that your reaction is normal. You just hope your reaction will help. Oh, you try to be a little more patient, try not to make the situation worse. But of course you know if you're pushed too far, you're allowed to blow up, because you're only human. And you get to decide what "too far" is for you, and they get to decide what "too far" is for them. Everyone thinks their own "too far" is patient and generous and everyone else's is short and selfish. No one knows any other way.

I learn all this just like we all do, simmering in my own family soup.

Then I get married and become my wife's husband. And then I become an alcoholic just like my dad. Three quarts of beer every day for fourteen years becomes another normal. I bring all my dysfunction and ignorance into my marriage, like we all do. And Brenda brings her whole story in too. And together we team up to learn more habits of just reacting, arguing, and being offended and defensive. Next stop: 1985.

How Can My Family Be Happy?

Twenty years earlier when I was a teenager, I started noticing, *It's pretty tense around here. Nobody seems very happy.* My younger brother and sister and I never have friends over. We never talk about why; we all just seem to understand it's not something you do. It's as if there's something inside our house that no one is supposed to see. The house is undisciplined. The dog poops on newspapers on the floor at the bottom of the stairs. There's no housekeeping. Dad sleeps in the basement family room. There's tension in the air. When Dad is home—shhhh—you need to be careful, and if he's not home, there's the risk he could come home any minute and who knows what mood he'll be in?

I realize something is missing in our home. It's a lack of peace, satisfaction, happiness. For a long time I don't notice, but as a fifteen-year-old, I am beginning to long for something I can't describe. I've never seen healthy family relationships, yet I sense there must be more than just knee-jerk reacting to people, arguing, getting offended, yelling, and protecting yourself.

A question is born in me: How can my family be happy?

A question is born in me: *How can my family be happy?* It seems there should be answers somewhere, a way out, some hope, some tools or something. But I don't know enough to even begin

25

to learn. I know I need enlightenment. As I grow older, I feel lost in a jungle of cluelessness. How can I get out of this jungle? I don't want to just leave it behind. I want to fix it.

We All Learn What's Normal as We Go

Around this same time, I know Mom and Dad struggle with money. So I say, "I'll do a budget for you!" I'm probably sixteen.

They give me their bills and income, we clear Dad's pile of papers and old mail off the kitchen table, and I go to work. Looking back, I'm sure they were humoring me, but I'm also sure they'd never actually done this before. I add it all up and go, "Uh, you don't have enough. You spend more than you make."

And they go, "Yeah, we know," and shrug.

And at that moment my eyes are opened to, *Oh, that's just the way it is. There's nothing you can do about it.*

It doesn't occur to anyone to actually deal with the financial situation. And so I learn to think that it's normal to believe you're stuck with how things are. Just accept it. The sky is blue, the grass is green, and if your family is unhappy, you have to learn to live with it.

At sixteen, I'm at an age where it's easy for dads and teenage sons to get into arguments, and we do. It's all part of growing up and finding your way. I think one motivation for our arguments is we both long to connect, but neither of us knows how. We just yell and argue as a substitute. "I love you" is not part of our vocabulary, but one time in mid-argument, I violate our unspoken code and blurt out, "Dad, I love you! Don't you know that?"

He can't handle it. He doesn't know how to deal with those words. I'm sure he had his own similar issues with his dad. He stammers, "What are you, gay or something?" Fifty years later, I still feel the clueless craziness of that answer.

He can't handle the potential intimacy. It's as if he's rejecting an opportunity to be happy. I think, *Saying I love you is a negative*

26

thing? To be avoided? Shouldn't saying I love you make people happy? How can I make us happy? I begin dating Brenda after high school while still living at home. I come home from dates and go downstairs to say hi to Dad. The family room is his bedroom, TV room, living room. He sleeps on the couch. The TV's on as usual. I'm getting serious about Brenda. But neither Dad nor I know how to talk about marriage or relationships or becoming an adult. We have these awesome opportunities to connect one-on-one, but neither of us knows what to do. So we just watch Johnny Carson and Benny Hill and Perry Mason reruns until 1:00 a.m. and make small talk about sports. That's it. No meaning or depth. I just want to connect, and I think he does too, but how? I assume this is just the way it is, so of course I accept it. But I don't like it. How can a family be happy?

I turn twenty-one, and he takes me to the Cozy Lounge for my first official drink as an adult. Hmm, not bad. Later, I start buying beer on my own. Then more. I discover something good—beer relieves the frustration and that lost-in-the-jungle feeling. How can a family be happy? I don't know, but maybe I'll think about it later.

Brenda and I get married. I am going to do my absolute best, everything I know how, to make her happy. But I don't know how. I never learned. *I'll just try to be what she wants me to be*, right? Ha! And I never can. I feel I always disappoint her. What's the secret? Add in that I become an alcoholic for fourteen years, drinking at least three quarts of beer every day. I learn more habits of just reacting and being defensive. And I lie to Brenda about how much I'm drinking.

We Humans Are Incredible Learning Machines

Without trying or realizing it, we all process our daily experiences and adapt our thinking and behavior to help us get through the day. I learn arguing is a great way to distract people from talking about things you don't want to hear. I learn that when you're wrongly accused, make sure you really give it back when that person does something wrong. How dare they accuse me! I learn to be outraged at unfairness against me, because in my mind my good far outweighs my bad, and so my good should be appreciated. I learn how to use being offended to manipulate people to back off. If someone can't see the light of the truth, then manipulation is justified, wouldn't you say?

> *All I'm doing is learning what doesn't work. Twenty years of what doesn't work.*

I end up thinking there's something wrong with me. I go to the local mental health clinic for enlightenment—we had a good one in our town. I explain to the counselor how I feel. Life isn't working, and I don't know how to be happy or have a happy family. What am I missing? I want him to understand and at least encourage me and give me hope. "Do you know what I mean?" I say.

He says, "No. I've never felt that way."

Now, I realize that to do his job he doesn't need to have ever felt like me, but still his response makes me feel hopeless and foolish. I feel like Charlie Brown in the Christmas special—except I'm saying, "Doesn't anyone know what family happiness is all about?"

I know there must be answers. There must be tools to use or ways to think so things make sense. But I'm clueless.

So now it's 1985.

I've been looking for this family happiness for almost twenty years. All I'm doing is learning what doesn't work. Twenty years of what doesn't work.

We've been married thirteen years, I'm thirty-five years old, and our oldest daughter is almost a teenager.

We take a family vacation to Texas to visit my brother. And Brenda makes a comment about something she thinks I'm doing and thinking. I'm *not* doing it, but I go into my full offended meltdown mode using everything I've learned.

"I can't believe you'd think that! I'm so tired of you believing things about me that aren't true! You always accuse me! Why do you always think the worst of me?"

It's a huge, overblown argument from me. The kids hear it all. I act like I've been *so* wronged, *so* offended. I'm persecuted, a victim.

Soon I feel shame over how I acted. But I can't take it back. Now I'm not mad; I'm just a horrible person. And part of the shame is that I know there *is* something I deserve blame for that she *isn't* criticizing, because I'm drinking way more beer than she realizes. I stay out way too long on errands so I can drink in the car without her knowing how much. And when she calls me on it, I get offended about that too.

"Why did it take you so long?"

"That's just how long it takes! This is normal!," I respond.

Over time she starts thinking maybe her thinking is cuckoo because she seems to be thinking things that aren't true. And I let her think it. *Yeah, you're ridiculous.*

I'm lying to her, breaking our intimacy, letting her think maybe it's her and that she's the one who's wrong—all so I can have my beer.

And then I get mad and offended at her for some little comment. What a horrible thing to do.

I can't make her happy. I don't know how to have a happy family. And it's not going to change.

Your Normal Can Change

Then three things happen:

1. I miraculously stop drinking.
2. Two years later, I believe in Jesus.
3. Six months after that I meet someone who mentors and shepherds me.

These three things change everything, each one piling on the previous one. It takes time and is still ongoing. But once your direction changes, certain things become inevitable. Get the direction right and good things will come.

I don't know how I stopped drinking. I didn't go to AA or Celebrate Recovery, and there was no family-and-friends intervention. There is a long period of guilt and frustration and trying to quit on my own. However, unknown to me, Brenda and her friends are praying. One day Brenda confronts me (again), and I'm so tired of lying and hiding I blurt out, "Brenda, I'm an alcoholic."

She doesn't get mad or argue. I wish she would, so I could argue back. Instead, I'm stuck with the realization that I just broke her heart. I'm stuck with my bad, lying, drinking self. It's too much. I know I won't drink another beer for a while. A while turns into decades. I'm now convinced Jesus got me sober to get me home to him.

Without beer I can think straight, and after two years of straight thinking, my soul becomes convinced that I'm lost, spiritually dead, and separated from God. That's bad news. One evening, alone in the basement of our rental house in Bettendorf, Iowa, I get down on my knees and give my life to Jesus. I say out loud, "Please take my life, I don't want it, I don't know what to do with it." That's good news.

Six months later, I meet the man who will mentor and shepherd me. He invites me to a class he's teaching at church. He posts a sign on the wall in front of the room. "Think Biblically," it says. Thinking biblically, he says, means learning to connect the dots. The dots are me, God, family, people, the world, and all our hopes and dreams. The more you see how the dots connect and fit together, the more life makes sense. The more you learn to cooperate with the connections, the easier things become. More good news.

The Bible becomes fascinating to me. The man, Harold, shows me how to apply the Bible to my life. I begin to unlearn some of those habits of defensiveness and emotional reacting. I begin to learn new perspectives and to understand how things work and why and how marriage and family relationships work and don't work. I read and study on my own and pay attention to people's words, behaviors, and attitudes. I learn that I really can do nothing apart from Jesus.

Not only do I learn the truth that's in the Bible, but I also begin soaking up the demeanor and personality behind the words. I hear God's tone of voice and feel his character of grace, humility, and patience. Slowly over time I sense that unique demeanor and personality of God working their way in and through me.

One Small Step, One Giant Leap

Brenda and I have been married close to twenty years by this time, and the kids are teenagers. I still get defensive, still get offended, still argue, still don't know how to make my family happy—but life is better. I feel softer. My trust in Jesus is growing. I'm putting down roots.

One day I'm talking to Harold about finances and debt and money. I never wanted debt and would never touch our savings. I didn't want to borrow money even to buy a house. We're renting with no plans to buy, and guess what? Brenda isn't happy. Harold makes it seem as if Brenda being happy is pretty important. He tells me there are worse things than mortgage debt and spending a little money on a house to make your wife happy. I trust Harold's judgment and think maybe I'm wrong.

I think, *So if I let Brenda buy some furniture from savings, I'm not violating the Bible?*

Uh, no.

And it makes her so happy! And that makes me happy, because I made her happy! She didn't even buy new furniture; she bought used! And she loved doing it. It was wonderful. She found beautiful, quality pieces that were so good we kept them for years.

I experience satisfaction in her satisfaction. This is a first. It's a breakthrough. She feels cared about. She feels loved. She feels like her feelings matter. I never expected this to make her feel so good. I enjoy her enjoyment. The atmosphere in our home changes.

And then our refrigerator breaks, and there's not enough money in the budget to buy a new one for two weeks. Harold says, "Well, I guess you don't need a refrigerator." Huh? How can we not need a fridge? Then I realize he's reminding me that God says he'll supply every need according to his riches in Christ. If he's not supplying it, we must not need it. He knows, he's in control, he supplies our needs, so trust him for a fridge.

Hmmm. I can understand that. It's called faith. We never had that in the home I grew up in. Instead, we panicked and got mad and felt shame.

Brenda agrees. OK, we'll use a cooler for a few weeks. Jesus is in control, so let's act like it.

Then I take a job in Texas, far away from our youngest daughter, who is in college and just beginning a relationship with the guy she'll marry. We're moving away, and Brenda is going to miss all the mother-daughter talks after the dates and leading up to the engagement. We're going to be over twelve hundred miles away. Brenda is going through her own issues of fear and insecurity, and she's crying several times a day.

Harold says to me, "When you get to Austin, put away your lists and concentrate on her."

I am to put her first and help her in her pain and insecurity. And I'm surprised to discover what a sweet, sweet assignment this is. I work early hours and get off at noon, so we can spend afternoons together exploring, shopping, and enjoying ourselves. It's too good.

It makes her happy. I made her happy! This is so satisfying!

Discovering the Lost Tools

Between the furniture, the refrigerator, and putting away my agenda, it's as if I'm discovering secret laws of the universe.

Jesus meets my needs! I don't have to be stingy and protect myself. I can be generous.

I can put the other person first and experience more satisfaction than when I put myself first.

Generosity is actually not a sacrifice. It feels good! It really *is* more blessed to give than receive. When I give, I actually get. And what I get is so good it almost feels selfish to give.

Cue the angels singing the "Hallelujah Chorus." Cue Dorothy, Toto, and friends dancing out of the woods and into the light. I've come out of the woods too. I'm enlightened. This is the beginning of a beautiful journey. I know the starting point for how to be happy. I know the starting point for how to make Brenda happy. I still have to go down the path—it's sometimes hard and I make mistakes—but at least I know the path to follow.

> It's as if I'm discovering secret laws of the universe.

These are the kinds of things that lead to a happy family.

It's backward. You lose your life to save it. If you grasp for it and for your "rights," you'll lose it, but if you release it, you'll keep it.

Refresh others and you'll be refreshed.

Generosity and caring and trusting Jesus feel good. They make other people feel good. People who feel good get along.

Life is never going to be fair, so somehow I give up expecting fairness. I do my best to trust Jesus to take care of me.

When you're caring and generous, people tend to respond likewise, but even if they don't, giving still feels good.

Sacrifice for them to make them happy, and you'll be happy.

Isn't this a law of the universe? God loves peace and reconciliation, and peace and reconciliation are achieved by sacrifice. Isn't this what Jesus did?

Of course, there's no guarantee that cooperating with this law will bring about the changes that Brenda and I experienced. There are exceptions, and those exceptions have their own purposes and lessons that God intends for good. But in general, honoring how the Lord made things to work will somehow, some way, and at some time, be honored by him in our experience.

> *God loves peace and reconciliation, and peace and reconciliation are achieved by sacrifice.*

I continue to call Harold weekly with questions about marriage, family, kids, finances, work, and church. I can't get enough of this new direction. I want more and more of what this enlightenment looks like in all the situations of every day. "Why does this happen? Now what do I do?" He rarely gives me straight answers but asks questions that help me think and see on my own.

I tell him, "I don't want to have to call you every time I have a question."

"You'll get there," he says.

I don't get there, but I go further than I could ever imagine. Learning to think biblically takes time, but it's slowly affecting the man I am becoming, the husband, dad, and family member.

Good-Bye, 1985

Our family becomes more and more unlike the family I grew up in and more unlike 1985.

The daughters get older and marry. Grandkids appear. Our entire family grows, evidenced by the ways we relate to each other, the grace and patience we extend to each other.

We assume the best, not the worst. We give each other the benefit of the doubt. We root for each other rather than manipulate to make ourselves feel better. We're genuinely curious about each other, and we accept each other as we are. We want what's best for each other without insisting on our own expectations. We have an unspoken agreement concerning decisions that says, "Relationships come first." There are no big divisions, no elephants in the room pushing us away from each other.

We have disagreements, but they're small elephants, and they don't dominate our attitudes and family atmosphere. There's no getting mad and stomping off and not talking for days or weeks or years. Grace and patience dominate. Trust in each other and in God dominates.

Unlike all those years ago, we now do things purposefully. We get together yearly for "Goals Weekend" to hear each other's heartbeat. Brenda and I hold "Grandy Camp" every year to reconnect with the grandkids without the moms and dads around. We share with each other about major decisions, expecting encouraging straight talk in return. Our family has grown into a safe place to launch and a soft place to land.

We're a long way from the old days of arguing, being defensive, taking offense, acting out of emotions, and repeating the same patterns over and over as if there is no other way.

People notice. They see Brenda and me and our relationship. They see our daughters and their marriages and families. They see us root for each other and get along. Our entire family legacy has changed. Sometimes they ask, "How do you do that?"

We do it by adopting simple attitudes, perspectives, expectations, and actions—the ones you see in the Bible, the ones Harold made real to me, the ones you know in your gut are true, right, and good. You can adopt them too. For a while, I called them the *Lost Tools of Family Peace and Happiness*, because for a long time they were lost to me. Today, however, they have become for me the *Timeless Tools of Family Peace*.

We also do it by moving away from all those old ways of thinking and living. I didn't know it at the time, but I had been following a very common playbook, one that's deeply ingrained in every human being. It's as if someone has created another set of tools designed to create family *dis*harmony. You're given those tools at birth. I call them the *Everyday Tactics of Family Disharmony*, and I was a master at them.

You can replace performance and manipulation in your family with acceptance and grace. It's not an impossible dream. It's what God wants, and he's calling us to cooperate and trust him while he achieves his goals and purposes in our lives and families. You can make a difference in your family. You can feel better about even your most challenging family relationships. You can replace the *Everyday Tactics of Family Disharmony* with the *Timeless Tools of Family Peace*. That's what this book is about.

We do it by adopting simple attitudes, perspectives, expectations, and actions. . . . You can adopt them too.

The way to begin is not by following a formula or checking off steps on a checklist. We begin by appreciating our family in its timelessness. If you were able to get every family member together and take a snapshot, you'd back way up to get everyone in. You'd think you have a picture of your family, but you don't. The ones you see are not the whole story. You have to back up even farther—generations—to get everyone in. You need a movie, not a snapshot. Your whole story is sweeping, boundless, impressive, and moving. Our families flow. Like a river. And you're in the middle of that river.

— 2 —

The River of Family
Your Role Is Bigger Than You Think

Destiny is not a matter of chance, it is a matter of
choice. It is not a thing to be waited for, it is a thing
to be achieved.

William Jennings Bryan

Driving east, two minutes before you get to the house of our daughter Myquillyn, you cross a shallow, rocky river. It's even called the Rocky River. It joins the Great Pee Dee and eventually flows into the Atlantic Ocean near Georgetown, South Carolina.

Our twelve-year-old grandson, Cademon, and I decide to have an adventure together and paddle several miles of the Rocky River in a canoe.

I don't know anything about canoes or floating on rivers. I don't know what to expect. I've only seen the river from the bridge. Will it get deep and wide somewhere? Are there rapids? Will we see eagles? Gators? Pirates? In my supercivilized world, this is the equivalent of an adventure to infinity and beyond.

We push off from another bridge a few miles upriver and wave good-bye to family members who will meet us later at the bridge near Myquillyn's house. Very quickly, it gets quiet. No houses, no vehicles, no roads, no people. Birds and insects sound like they're roaring in the stillness.

We get to where the river flows over a stretch of rocks—noisy, fast, and shallow. We get stuck, get out, and push the canoe a few yards past the rocks. Instantly, we know we are wimps. We don't need a class or a guide to tell us we've violated a code of the river. Real canoers don't get out and push. They *navigate*.

After several more areas of rocky rapids, we've got it down. First, before we can see it, we hear the sound of the rapids up ahead. We look until we see where the line of fast water begins, and we search for a section where the water is flowing fast and deep through the rocks. We aim for that spot, paddle *faster* not slower, and zoom through the rapids. No one tells us this is the way to do it; we just know instinctively, as if it's ingrained in our human muscle memory, passed down from generations who depended on boats the way we depend on cars.

We drift again, listen to the buzz of mosquitos, shoot another rapids, then drift again in silence.

Even though our section of the river is an adventure to us, we know the river starts way before we got in.

And the river ends way after we get out.

Just like our families.

Let's Turn Our Hearts Downriver

We think of family as the ones we see now, along with those gone before us whose memories and stories we share. But our families are bigger than that. Your entire family, going back generations, is a mighty river. Upriver goes back further than any scrapbook can hold. We can't see that far. We only know that this spot in the river came from back there.

We can't see very far downriver either. We can't get high enough to see where it ends; we only know that what's in this spot today will keep flowing in that direction.

We are a part of something much bigger than us, even though the section of river we're in right now seems plenty big. We paddle this part the best we can, usually without schooling or guides, learning to navigate the rapids as we go.

One of the many rapids in my family? My great-grandfather abandoned his family. Then, years later, one of his sons killed himself.

I don't know the whole story. I only heard references to it, and I never asked any questions. I guess I thought it was none of my business. Today, I think the story could have served as a meaningful connection between family members sharing grief and life lessons. But, like many families, we didn't bring up shameful or bad things. I assembled the pieces over the years from cryptic comments made by family members who knew more than they wanted to say.

My dad was twelve years old, living with his mom and his dad, Pop (my grandfather). Pop also supported his brother and his mom, who lived with them. One Sunday everyone except Pop's brother went to church. When they got home, they couldn't open his bedroom door. Something was wedged against it. Closing that bedroom door was the last thing he did while he was alive. Was his suicide related to Pop's dad abandoning his family years earlier when Pop and his brother were kids? Who knows. But the influence of the abandonment was still being felt decades later in my

If we can blame our mom or dad or anyone else in our immediate family for how things turned out, they can do the same.

family growing up. My kid sister would get upset with our dad, and Mom would tell her, "Don't be too mad at your dad. Look who raised him—a guy who felt rejected and didn't have anyone to raise *him*."

When Pop became an adult, he changed the spelling of our last name to forever separate himself from his dad, as if to say, "Since you wanted to leave, you're never coming back. You won't find us." The echo of this is heard generations later every time I spell our name for someone: "That's M-O-R-L-A-N-D with no E."

But it's only an echo. Our family was not destined to a straight-line repetition and payment for one person's sin. Your family isn't either. The consequences of what happened upriver have altered our family, but they have not trapped us into a destiny.

Your parents and family are in the boat with you. You get into a family that's already flowing. They had parents and a family too, and on back it goes. If we can blame our mom or dad or anyone else in our immediate family for how things turned out, they can do the same. If we pass something upriver, they can too. And on back upriver the blame goes.

Much of what our families become is because we're part of what has gone before. We can't escape it:

"I may _____, but so did my dad; I learned it from him."
   True.

"My parents never taught me _____." True.

"My mom never showed me _____." True.

"My dad never _____; he always just _____." True.

"My uncle _____ me, and so now I'm _____." True.

These things are all true, and they may have affected us and changed the course of our lives. But if I *blame* my family, and push responsibility for who and what I am onto them, the blame can go all the way upriver.

It goes downriver too. From Brenda and me, through Myquillyn and Chad and Emily and John, through their kids and families, and their kids' kids and families, the river flows. Each of them could pass the blame back to Brenda and me.

Most of us probably don't consciously blame previous generations for how we turned out. But it's a very subtle temptation because it gives us an excuse for our faults and failures. It takes a lot of courage to face who we are and a great deal of responsibility to deal with it. Blame lightens the load a little bit, doesn't it? Saying to yourself "If only this hadn't happened" sometimes makes life more bearable.

> *We put a canoe into this family story when we are born, and our canoe pulls to shore when we die.*

But blame is irrelevant. It only matters if you want an excuse for not taking responsibility for yourself.

It is helpful to understand the things that have contributed to your story, to what happened in your family upriver. These things may help to explain who you are today. But it is your fault alone if you allow those circumstances to keep you from being all you can be.

You can stop the chain reaction. Accept your family (or lack of one) as within God's overall will for you, and accept his ability—and promise—to use it for good. Then let him.

My dad's dad (Pop) was an alcoholic. My dad was an alcoholic. I am an alcoholic. My children are *not* alcoholics. If God can stop that chain with me, he can stop whatever is plaguing you with you.

All we have is our part of the river, right here, right now. We put a canoe into this family story when we are born, and our canoe pulls to shore when we die.

But what we do while in the river—our actions, attitudes, words, values, accomplishments—will roll on. They are our legacy. We can navigate the part of the river we're in right now and influence—for good or bad—what flows downriver from here. One of the things we can pass on is our example of not assessing blame.

Victor Hugo is often quoted as saying, "To reform a man, you must begin with his grandmother." Let's start the reforming with us. Purposefully or not, we're casting drops of our legacy into the current that is flowing downriver. Let's do more on purpose.

> *We can navigate the part of the river we're in right now and influence—for good or bad—what flows downriver from here.*

When I was young, the home of my grandfather "without the E" was very different from the home I grew up in. This was after Pop's alcoholic days. It was calm, orderly, quite a contrast to ours, and I noticed. Our house was stressful and chaotic. Theirs felt peaceful and normal. I think they showed me peaceful and normal on purpose.

We washed windows and made iced tea. We did the dishes and put them away. We weeded the garden in the yard and gathered its produce. These were little oasis moments in a little oasis place with kind oasis people.

A bit of purposeful, oasis-making reform can start with anyone. It doesn't have to be a grandmother. It can be a mom. Or a dad, brother, sister, daughter-in-law, cousin, or it could be you. Maybe the best time to start was generations ago way back upriver, but the next best time to start is now. Today can be a drop of grace into your family that flows and never ends.

Let's Let God Prove Something

The Cuyahoga River in Cleveland became famous for being so polluted it frequently caught fire. People said it didn't flow; it oozed. They said you couldn't drown in the river; you decayed. Maybe that's how you feel about part of your family river. Maybe you even feel like your river makes the Cuyahoga look like a sparkling stream. Imagine then, one morning when your river is feeling especially muddy, you open your mailbox and find something special.

It's a gold-embossed invitation to a recognition ceremony. A Hall of Fame induction. You see the names of the inductees, and you can't believe *you've* been invited! They are rock stars of history and heroes in God's kingdom, and you get to see them in person. You go through all the preparation and arrive early. Things begin with a dramatic orchestral buildup, a fanfare, and finally the ceremony starts with a long, passionate standing ovation.

For?

The twelve tribes of Israel. The original twelve siblings. Jacob's kids. The family that the nation of Israel came from. Live and in person. You're on your feet, right?

Before they're introduced, a video of the life and times of the inductees reviews why they're so worthy of honor.

You see a momma's boy named Jacob lying to his dad, then running for his life from his brother. He ends up living with his uncle and falls in love with the uncle's daughter, Rachel. He works seven years for the right to marry her but at the last minute is tricked into marrying her sister, Leah. Jacob works seven more years for the right to marry Rachel. He doesn't love Leah and she knows it, so she hopes having a child will give her favor over her sister. Reuben is born, but nope, no love from Jacob. Leah scores again with a second child, Simeon. Then Levi, then Judah, and now it's four to nothing, Leah over Rachel.

But Leah still doesn't feel the love, and now Rachel doesn't either and is jealous because her sister has children and she doesn't. Rachel breaks out her secret weapon, her maid Bilhah, who then has two kids by Jacob, Dan and Naphtali. Rachel's catching up! Leah pulls the same trick with her maid Zilpah, and Gad and Asher are born. The drama continues with bribes and trickery and jealousy and substitute moms, and finally Rachel conceives! Joseph and Benjamin end the baby wars.

There's the honorable beginning of your twelve tribes of Israel. And there's more. You see debauchery and murder and near-genocide, and one of them gets his daughter-in-law pregnant thinking she's a prostitute. The brothers gang up on a younger sibling, plot a first-degree murder, then decide to sell him into slavery instead; they go back home and tell Dad he's dead, breaking his heart for decades. The shameful, scandalous introductory video goes on, leaving you and the audience numb and slack-jawed.

Then it's time for the twelve sons to appear in person. Do you stand and cheer now? I'm thinking something changes in the mood and response at the ceremony. How did these guys get this place of honor? What are they doing anywhere near this building? They're no better than anybody else! Maybe worse!

You would think that if God was going to choose a people to make himself known, a people who would be a blessing to the whole world, who would guard his name and reputation, and who would eventually give the world a savior, he'd be rather picky. If you were God, you'd probably engineer things so that this family was the best. There's a lot at stake.

And that's when it hits you. It's not them; it's what was done with them despite them being them. There *is* someone who deserves recognition for making something so incredibly glorious out of this train wreck of a family. Where is he so we can give him the credit and honor and glory that we thought these guys deserved?

He walks out on the stage and receives everything due him. He looks at each one in the audience—and right at you—and says, "How messed up are you? How dysfunctional is your family? Is it worse than this family that I used for royal business? I can do the same with and for you. Will you let me prove something through your family? Will you let me show you how I can bring something good out of your family situation too?"

How do you think you'd feel when you got home from such a ceremony—part of something big, something grand? That's a good feeling. How does God go about this "something big"?

1. He often starts with family.

In the beginning is God himself: God says he is the Father and Jesus is his Son. They have a family relationship. Then God creates a nation to bring his Son, the Savior, into the world. That nation starts with the family of Abraham, and God makes a promise to that nation. When he fulfills the promise, he starts again with *another* family. The Son of God is born into a family with a mom and a dad, brothers and sisters. Family is a big deal to God, and your family is part of that big deal. Family is his idea, he loves and delights in it, and he works through it for his glory.

> A river touches places of which its source knows nothing, and Jesus says if we have received of His fullness, however small the visible measure of our lives, out of us will flow the rivers that will bless to the uttermost parts of the earth.
>
> Oswald Chambers[1]

2. He starts small and allows time for growth.

The work Jesus came to do would be done by the adult Jesus. Why start with a baby? Why take thirty years to get him to adulthood? Isn't that a waste of time? Isn't it risky? Why put him on the same path as every human ever born? Shouldn't he be an exception? Why choose the slow way for such an important mission?

God must take great pleasure in patience and in taking time to let a family grow.

Is what you see small and baby-sized and far from adulthood? Are your expectations for change and growth in your family, or with that certain person, more aggressive than God's? Are you in a bigger hurry for progress in your most challenging family relationships than God was for human-kind's redemption?

3. He uses unimposing, common leftovers.

Jesus entered the world in a place where animals were born and fed. Do you think one of the first things he smelled was straw and dung? Straw is what's left when the good stuff's taken out, and dung is too. Can you have a more unimposing, common beginning than that? Your family's problems, issues, and limitations may stink, but probably not more than the stink in that stable. And Jesus was put there *on purpose. By God.*

So if your river seems hopelessly muddy, and relief in your most challenging relationships seems far off and stagnant, you're in good company. That's how God saved the world.

Helpful Bonuses for You

Free bonuses are available online right now, including a worksheet to use as you get into the practical application portions of this book. You can fold it up and keep it between the pages to help you with note-taking to make the most of what you read.

Just visit afamilyshapedbygrace.com/bookbonus. You'll find free printable versions of what's coming up in the next chapter:

- The Family Satisfaction Assessment and Worksheet
- An expanded version of the What I Want to See list to help you through the rest of the book
- The Family Peace Polestar Printable

Plus you can get printable worksheets and printouts of many of the tools and lists in the book.

You'll also find more connections, resources, and surprises to go deeper and to help apply the message of this book and make it real in your family relationships.

Visit afamilyshapedbygrace.com/bookbonus.

— 3 —

Rollin' Down Your River

Where You Are Now, What You Want, and What It Can Look Like

> Not everything that is faced can be changed. But nothing can be changed until it is faced.
>
> James Baldwin

There was a moment after I first met Harold when he told me, "You could call me." It was an invitation to connect with him to answer questions and make theoretical things real in my life. I had a choice. Call or don't call. Get some answers or keep going the way I was.

What if he tells me something I don't want to hear? What if I have to change something I'm doing? Maybe thinking about change is enough.

I called. That was the beginning of understanding I had choices— choices to adopt simple attitudes, perspectives, and expectations.

Then I had the choice to learn to think and behave consistently with those new attitudes, perspectives, and expectations. Over the next ten years, I called him hundreds of times. He called me maybe three or four times. He would not chase me. I had to want it. If I didn't want it, I would not make the commitment to the change I said was needed. If I had not made that choice, if I had not started calling him, if I had not chosen to put myself under his influence, I don't believe you would be reading this right now. It would still be 1985.

By reading this far you have made a choice to put yourself under the influence of the same simple attitudes and perspectives that changed me. But that's just the beginning. I planted grass recently, and the beginning was loosening the soil, raking it smooth, spreading the seed, and then watering it. That was work, but if I'd stopped there, the grass wouldn't have grown. I had to water it regularly for several weeks, sometimes several times a day. Beginning wasn't enough. The grass needed my commitment.

My conversations with Harold became like a class, but the curriculum was my own personal life and issues. I ended up with a shelf of three-ring binders and manila file folders filled with notes. That was part of the evidence of my commitment.

You don't need binders and folders and pages of notes. Well, a piece of paper or two might help—we'll get to that in a minute. But you do have to make a commitment to adopt the same simple attitudes, perspectives, expectations, and actions that my family and I have adopted and that have made such a difference to us.

This commitment will impact your most challenging family relationships. It will influence how you see people and interpret their behavior, which will then influence how you feel. Then you will learn how to live in a way that is consistent with your new attitudes and perspectives in your everyday relationships. Over time you will learn to replace habitual emotional reactions with purposeful ones. Over time you will feel better, and your entire family will change.

This commitment does not need to add to your day. It's a commitment in your heart and mind. You're not adding things; you're adjusting how you think and speak and act.

This book will help you adopt those simple attitudes, perspectives, expectations, and actions. Harold never used this phrase, but I do now when I call those attitudes and actions the *Timeless Tools of Family Peace*—these are the same tools that were previously lost to me. Once you see the list of these tools, you'll return to it again and again. But a list isn't enough; you need guidance.

So I'll try to guide you on which ones are most important for *your* family. You'll learn to know what's normal, what to expect. You'll learn simple steps to take. You'll learn how to relate and respond depending on the person and situation. You'll learn to rediscover the *Timeless Tools* yourself and see what they can look like in your unique family relationships.

So Let's Get Started!

In this chapter, we'll begin with how you currently feel about your family relationships. Then you'll picture how you'd like any challenging relationships to change. Finally, we'll envision what this all can add up to and see if it looks good to you.

This will be fun, and the results and your reaction will prepare you to personalize this book as much as possible. Think of this chapter as a warm-up exercise. You're stretching before you begin paddling.

Where You Are Now

You're going to take the Family Satisfaction Assessment. It's easy and quick. But first, here are a few definitions:

Family: For the purposes of this book and assessment, your family is your spouse, children, brothers and sisters, parents, in-laws, grandparents, aunts, uncles, cousins, and step-everythings. Whatever relatives are your greatest sources of pleasure, pain, and concern, that's who we're considering to be your family.

Challenging relationship: This is any relationship with a relative that you struggle with and are sometimes preoccupied with. It doesn't matter where they live or how they're related to you; if they're involved in a painful relationship with you or someone else in your family and it bothers you, then that's a challenging relationship for you. If you see someone only once a year, but it's a painful one time a year, that's a challenging relationship for you. You decide *how* challenging it is.

The Family Satisfaction Assessment: This assessment is not an evaluation of your family or your relationships. Rather, it's a simple tool to help you understand *how you feel* about your family relationships. Got it? It's not about them; it's about you and what you think and feel.

There are only five questions. Keep track of your responses, add them up, and find your score at the end. Then I'll have a few more questions to help you narrow down which challenging relationship(s) you can focus on for the rest of this book. You can also download a printable version of this assessment at afamily shapedbygrace.com.

Family Satisfaction Assessment

1. Compared to what you'd like to see, how do you currently feel about the condition of your family relationships *overall*, in your entire family?

awesome				OK, decent				not good at all		
10	9	8	7	6	5	4	3	2	1	0

2. Most families have some areas of wonderful relationships as well as some areas of challenging relationships. From your perspective, in the last five years, how have *the most challenging family relationships* in your family changed?

way, way better				no change				way, way worse		
10	9	8	7	6	5	4	3	2	1	0

3. How hopeful are you that any further improvement needed in those challenging relationships *will* happen?

super hopeful			neither hopeful nor discouraged			super discouraged				
10	9	8	7	6	5	4	3	2	1	0

4. How confident are you that you can personally make a difference in the quality of your most challenging family relationships? (Don't overspiritualize this with, "I can do nothing; it's all Christ." That's true. Billy Graham could do nothing either; it was all Christ. But when he got up to speak, he made a difference. Think of the question in that way.)

very confident			neutral, don't know			no confidence at all				
10	9	8	7	6	5	4	3	2	1	0

5. In the most challenging family relationships referred to in questions 2 and 3, what are the relationships? (Step relationships are included and not counted separately.) Who are they with? See the following list. You can check more than one to include as your *most* challenging relationships:

Spouse

Children at home

Grown children

Your siblings (yes, stepsiblings too)

Between siblings at home

Between siblings outside your home
Parents
Mother-in-law
Daughter-in-law
Father-in-law
Son-in-law
Family on spouse's side
Former spouse
Former spouse's new spouse and family
Grandparents
Aunts, uncles, cousins
Other

Got one or a few checked? Got your score from the first four questions?

32 or above = You are feeling really good and satisfied, and I want to read the book you should write. Where is your lowest score? That's were there's room for even more satisfaction.

24–31 = You are definitely more satisfied than discouraged, and with a few adjustments you could feel awesome.

16–23 = You are between satisfied and discouraged and could lean either way, and you could easily become more satisfied with some consistent adjustments.

15 and below = You're definitely more discouraged than satisfied, but be encouraged because this means even small improvements could make a dramatic, encouraging difference to you.

The point of this simple assessment is to bring to the surface your feelings about your family and your expectations and hopes for change. You already have these feelings and expectations, but you don't usually think about them. Dust them off with one of those little microfiber polishing cloths and wear them like a pair of eyeglasses as you read this book. By doing so, everything you read in the book will be through the lens of your own feelings about and hopes for your challenging family relationships.

Maybe you agree with this statement: "I'm pretty happy with my family relationships overall, but one or two are very challenging to me." If so, imagine how great you'll feel when you make even a little progress in those one or two relationships.

Or maybe you agree with this statement: "One or more of my family relationships are so challenging to me that they are negatively affecting my entire experience of family." If so, imagine feeling more satisfied in your experience of family—not perfect, but better. That can be a fantastic result from improving just one or two relationships.

This book will show you not only that you can feel better *and* make a difference but also how to get there.

This is your starting point. You're becoming more conscious of what you already feel and expect. You have an idea of your satisfaction level with your entire family as well as with certain challenging relationships. You realize how much or how little confidence you have about making improvements in those relationships. And you have in mind one or more specific relationships that are most challenging to you.

What Do You Want?

Now, you can do one more thing to get even more specific about what you'd like to see change. Writing things down helps solidify them and helps to make the thing you want more real. It implies a commitment to taking something seriously. So let's write. The words may be few, but they will be words filled with meaning and hope.

You can do this any way you'd like. One way is to write directly in the space provided. Or you may get an expanded, printable version at afamilyshapedbygrace.com to use as a note-taking companion as you read.

This is not a to-do list. Instead, it's more of a personal sensitivity list. It's not something you're going to work on. We don't "work on" people. These are family members you love. You simply want to be open to seeing something or adjusting your attitude or discovering one thing you can do that might make a difference.

> *You simply want to be open to seeing something or adjusting your attitude or discovering one thing you can do that might make a difference.*

You're choosing to be purposeful.

Think of the relationships and people who came to mind during your assessment. For now, limit the number of names you write down to not more than three, so this exercise won't feel overwhelming. To begin, you will be learning some new habits of thinking and acting, and you don't want to be burdened by too many people to think about. Pick the three relationships in which improvement would make the biggest difference to you. If you have only one or two names, that's even simpler. The change in those relationships will affect others.

Write each name and very briefly describe what you would like to see and feel in your relationship with each person. You may be tempted to skim over this part and simply write a general desire and move on. *Don't.* Bring your deep desires for this person and this relationship to the surface. You are worth it. He or she is worth it. Remember, there is power in writing something down. It forces you to articulate your feelings. You're not to dredge up unpleasant words and scenes from the past; you are only to write *what you want in the future.* Pretend someone promised you that they would bring about whatever you want in this relationship— what would you say?

Avoid paragraphs; use words or short phrases. Let's call this your What I Want to See list.

Name _____
Words and phrases that describe what I'd love to see and feel in our relationship:

_____

_____

_____

_____

Name _____
Words and phrases that describe what I'd love to see and feel in our relationship:

_____

_____

_____

_____

Name _____
Words and phrases that describe what I'd love to see and feel in our relationship:

_____

_____

_____

_____

These are the people and the hopes that will be on your mind as you read this book. Just going through the process of writing these down has already begun to sensitize you to them. Later, you'll have a chance to go deeper and learn exactly the kinds of things to do that can bring the relief and improvement that you desire in these relationships.

Want to Aim Higher?

Now let's go even larger. When you think of the river of your family and the kind of family you'd like to see flowing downstream and gathering momentum into future generations, what do you see? If you're like I was, you've never thought of that. There was a time when I couldn't describe what I wanted with my immediate family, let alone see our lives as part of a mighty river.

However, now I can describe what I want to see in the future. It's what my family and I aim at in our everyday relationships. What an encouragement it would have been if I had been able to see this when I first formed the question, "How do you have a happy family?" I would have known what a happy family could look like. I still would not have known how to get there, but I would have at least known what to shoot for. I've mentioned the simple attitudes, perspectives, and expectations that I learned from Harold and adopted over time. These are now so ingrained in my family that we never talk about them. We instinctively know if any of us violates them. What are they? When adopted, what does your family look like?

> *I believe that, ultimately, we are all looking for peace in our families.*

I call the following principles the Family Peace Polestar. The position of a polestar remains fixed in the night sky even though the earth is rotating. It's a dependable indicator of direction when navigating in the middle of the ocean. I believe that, ultimately, we are all looking for peace in our families.

This is the big picture. What are the values, scenes, feelings, and outcomes you want to aim for? The more your family looks like this, the more peace you'll experience in your relationships. Small progress in just a few areas can make a life-changing difference.

Life isn't this simple, but we need a simple place to start.

To know what you're aiming at isn't enough, however. Part 2 of this book shows you how to head in the direction of the Family Peace Polestar.

THE FAMILY PEACE ⭐ POLESTAR

AS A FAMILY SHAPED BY GRACE, TOGETHER, WITH GOD . . .

 We will become a family that roots for each other, replacing performance and manipulation with acceptance and grace, becoming a safe place to launch and a soft place to land.

 We will grow in becoming a calming influence, helping each other feel honored and valued, through the power of patient trust and attention.

 We will rise above feeling rejected, offended, or unappreciated by recognizing our value as God's divinely appointed hidden treasure in our family.

 We will soften hard hearts over time through the potency of small drops of grace, wooing more and scolding less.

 We will awaken to the highest potential of those around us by knowing the difference between God's expectations for them and ours.

 We will do this not only for the family in our own house but also for our relationships with parents, grown kids, siblings, step-family, in-laws, and out-laws.

 We will leave this world a better place because of the influence of our family spreading the power of love, of grace, and of rooting for each other.

Here's What Momentum Can Look Like

Together, in part 2, we'll be reminded of the power and peace of acceptance. When I recall how God has accepted me unconditionally, I gain a peace and a security that free me to accept my family unconditionally.

When they feel fully accepted by me, they soften and open up to me. When they open up and I pay attention, I hear what God is up to in their lives. My curiosity and attention cause them to feel valued, and they trust and open up even more.

As I hear what God is up to in their lives, I embrace being God's access to them, and I try to cooperate with God's vision for each one. Instead of scolding and criticizing, I encourage and woo, modeling what I want to see rather than repeatedly telling.

Slowly, the atmosphere of harmony, grace, and love spreads. No matter how long it takes or what results I see, I release control of those results to God, knowing that he loves my family and wants what's best for them even more than I do. I also trust him for what's best for me, which takes me back to where I started—remembering God's unconditional love for and acceptance of me. As I continue living in this way, momentum begins in them and in me.

But First

Before we begin building momentum, we're going to make ourselves aware of what we're up against. We all confront obstacles, the rocks and boulders that have accumulated in our river over the years. The challenges in our family relationships have been building for a long time. Our attitudes and actions have been a part of our family river for so long that we no longer notice them as part of the rushing current. We crash into them as we always have. They've become habits that have contributed to the rocky, dangerous river we're in now.

In the next chapter, as we look at these obstacles, we'll keep in mind the polestar and the people and desires we listed in the assessment. We'll courageously confront these rocks and boulders that are in the way of what we desire in our family relationships. It took me twenty years to realize what didn't work and that I had other choices. You might realize it in the time it takes you to read the next chapter. This could be painful because in addition to seeing your family members you will also see yourself. The good news is that it's just you and me here. No one else will see us wincing. I won't point a finger at your obstacles, and you don't point a finger at mine, OK?

> *Our attitudes and actions have . . . become habits that have contributed to the rocky, dangerous river we're in now.*

— 4 —

The Rocky River

The Everyday Tactics of Family Disharmony

For my people have committed two evils: they have forsaken me, the fountain of living waters, and hewed out cisterns for themselves, broken cisterns that can hold no water.

Jeremiah 2:13

Let's Get the Bad News Out of the Way

This chapter has the potential to be a downer and to result in some anger toward others and self-condemnation.

Don't let that happen.

It could also be a forehead-slapper like it was for me: "Wow! I never knew . . ." I almost laughed—but not quite—when I realized I'd been cluelessly digging a hole all those decades.

Before plotting your course for any trip you take, you first have to know where you are, right? Let this chapter help you find the "You Are Here" arrow so you can move on.

This chapter is about those things that get in the way of having the satisfying family relationships you desire. It's about the things that have helped create the unsatisfying relationships in the first place. These are the main obstacles. Rather than considering such things as anger or pride, which are givens, let's try to picture the specific attitudes and behaviors that have gotten us into trouble. Let's not keep them at arm's length. Let's be reminded why they're so persistent.

In my mind, I refer to the *Everyday Tactics of Family Disharmony* as the *Seven Deadly Sins*, which has helped me to experience the sorrow that "brings repentance" (2 Cor. 7:10 NIV). These are the opposite of the *Timeless Tools* I referred to earlier. The *Everyday Tactics* are not lost at all but are found (meaning, used) in most families. They prevent and can be deadly to peace.

I Bet These Will Surprise You

These *Everyday Tactics of Family Disharmony* don't seem all that bad. They're common, everyday occurrences, but their deep, negative impact is highly underestimated. To the degree these tactics are mastered, they can result in a family characterized by stress, lack of trust, defensiveness, arguments, and more.

We're all born with a deeply ingrained drive to find fulfillment, to feel loved and worthy.

When I was growing up, this was how my family lived. This was normal. We didn't know any other way. My dad modeled it, then I modeled it. And still I wondered why my family wasn't happy.

The *Everyday Tactics of Family Disharmony* come naturally to almost everyone because they help us to feel good about ourselves and to look good to others. We're all born with a deeply ingrained drive to find fulfillment, to feel loved and worthy. So on the surface, these tactics seem to give us the results we're seeking.

The trouble is they work so well that we can never stop using them. They never wear out. We can use the same tactic over and over or switch to another to find just the right combination to achieve the results we want. Most of us do this intuitively.

> *The more I trust that nothing can separate me from Jesus's love . . . the less I will depend on these tactics.*

Like the sacrifices in the Old Testament, the tactics result in only temporary fixes that don't solve the real problem. I now realize that I go to these tactics whenever I fail to trust the sufficiency of Jesus for my worth and value. The pressures that cause me to resort to these tactics are intended rather to lead me to Christ. The more I trust that nothing can separate me from Jesus's love—that he will never leave me, that he will work everything for my good, that he is in ultimate control of every situation—the less I will depend on these tactics.

For a long time, I had no ability to trust him because I didn't know him or believe in him. I was lost and dead to everything he is. The *Everyday Tactics of Family Disharmony* were my only option. Even after believing and *wanting* to trust him, trusting can still be difficult. For one thing, I've developed a lifelong habit of utilizing these tactics. And every Christian at some time in life experiences doubt that Jesus is truly sufficient for every obstacle, pain, problem, loss, and disaster. Trust in Jesus changes everything, but it may take time getting there.

The Journey Is Every Day

Daily, God allows circumstances that should cause me to trust him, but those same circumstances can tempt me to instead rely on my own ability. In Bible talk, it's the battle between the Spirit and the flesh, right here in our everyday family relationships. The *Everyday Tactics of Family Disharmony* are the flesh. No one taught me how to use them. I learned in an environment where they were practiced, and I "caught" them, like a cold or the flu. In fact, you could say they're contagious. They don't cure our need for affirmation; they only fight off the symptoms.

> God allows circumstances that should cause me to trust him, but those same circumstances can tempt me to instead rely on my own ability.

As you read through the list of tactics, you'll probably recognize many people, either in your family or in the mirror. Don't feel too bad. You're not alone. I'm adept at #1 and #7. But hopefully over time we'll abandon them more and more and replace them with the *Timeless Tools of Family Peace*. We may never escape these seven tactics, but we can keep them from being our normal way of life.

The *Everyday Tactics of Family Disharmony*

Tactic #1: Using Your Family to Attain the Inner Peace and Affirmation Only Jesus Can Provide

By a single offering he has perfected for all time those who are being sanctified. (Heb. 10:14)

In him the whole fullness of deity dwells bodily, and you have been filled in him, who is the head of all rule and authority. (Col. 2:9–10)

Inner peace always trumps external peace, but inner peace requires truly believing in the sufficiency of Jesus. It seems easier to get the affirmation and approval I need from those around me. So I very subtly manipulate people and their responses to get what I want. It begins with that voice I hear in my head saying things like:

I've got to take care of myself.

I've got to be right.

It's up to me to prove my worth.

If my family, or anyone in my family, looks bad, then I look bad.

There's not enough love to go around; I've got to get my share.

If I don't get affirmation here, where will I get it?

The manipulation is so subtle and feels so normal that I never realize I'm using my family as my source of deepest peace. But it's deadly to my influence in my family. I can't meet their needs and mine at the same time. I have to choose.

This is the foundational tactic of the *Everyday Tactics of Family Disharmony*, the one that all the others build on. But people who have inner peace through trusting in the sufficiency of Jesus don't need any of the tactics. They can be wronged, offended, or not get their way, yet not feel insecure. When this first tactic of disharmony is abandoned, all the others begin to fall away.

Using your family for what only Jesus can provide makes life all about you. When you use family members for something they can't possibly give, they're destined to fail you every time. One of the most meaningful things my wife ever said to me was her confession, "Poor man, I was trying to use you as Jesus for me." She had seen the light, and the day she said that was the day the pressure dropped off me and the day our relationship changed.

> When you use family members for something they can't possibly give, they're destined to fail you every time.

The more you trust in the personal sufficiency of Jesus, the better you feel about yourself and the less you need the approval of others.

Tactic #2: Practicing Performance-Based Acceptance (PBA)

If people don't jump through the hoop of pleasing me, they don't get the prize of my love, acceptance, or approval. I don't want to be nice to them. It's an awesome way to get people to do what I want, since everyone wants love, acceptance, approval, and a smile.

See how this tactic is connected to tactic #1? Without finding sufficiency in Jesus, deep in my soul I think I get only what I deserve. So I'll only give you what I think you deserve.

Again, it feels so normal I hardly realize I'm doing it. Others do the same with me when they make me the one who needs to perform for them, and that feels normal too. I actually don't mind much, because it feels like I'm in control of being accepted; all I need to do is perform. Trouble is, when it doesn't work, I get mad at them and judge myself a failure. But that's OK; I just switch tactics.

This is the way the world works, but it's the opposite of Jesus's way and the opposite of grace.

Performance-based acceptance is all about me. I set the standard others must meet to gain my acceptance.

The more I trust in the personal sufficiency of Jesus, the less I need to manipulate others, because I've learned that the power of unconditional love is far stronger.

Tactic #3: Keeping Score

Keeping score is another way the world works. I use this tactic to keep track of how often others wrong me. I keep track of how many times they've been against me, how much I've had to put up with, and how many times they've accused me of being wrong when I've been right. I hear myself, and them, arguing over who's right, who's worse, or who's remembering correctly. We each find ourselves thinking or saying:

I can't believe you did/said/thought that!
You never _____!

You always _____!
Sure I may _____, but at least I don't _____!

I keep track only of the wrongs of others, not my own. I tally what they owe me, not how I've hurt them.

This tactic is perfect for disrupting family peace, since we each act in the same way, keeping track of wrongs against us and feeling that others owe us something. If this goes on for years, we end up accumulating enough to hate each other.

Keeping score is all about you and how much others owe you. They are expected to change and make amends first because they're worse than you. You know this because you've kept score.

The more you trust in the personal sufficiency of Jesus for your heart, soul, and emotions, the less you need to keep score to feel better about yourself or to look good, because you already have what you need.

Tactic #4: Rejecting and Marginalizing

Tactic #4 is usually related to performance-based acceptance (PBA). I use it to make myself feel better and make others feel worse. In my mind, I'm just being fair and giving what's deserved, but I use it when I feel that I can't win.

Rejection doesn't have to be overt; it can be subtly withholding myself from others—and I don't mind if they sense it. I act like I don't care and give them the cold shoulder. I act politely but never use more words than necessary and never ask a sincere question.

Rejecting and marginalizing are perfect for intimidating others and teaching them not to challenge me, which could lead to me being confronted with unpleasant things about myself. No one likes being rejected or marginalized, so they will usually treat me in ways that keep me from doing it.

Rejecting and marginalizing are all about you. You set the standard, make the judgment, and carry out the sentence.

The more you trust in the personal sufficiency of Jesus, the less you need to reject and marginalize others to look good and feel better about yourself, because Jesus satisfies those needs.

Tactic #5: Scolding, Criticizing, and Finding Fault

It's easy to notice when someone else constantly corrects or criticizes people. It's not as evident when I'm the one doing it.

The scolding, criticizing, and fault-finding tactic has been in use ever since the first fault-finder criticized and found fault with God in front of Adam and Eve. When I use this tactic habitually, I'm imitating the original critic.

Using this tactic with PBA and keeping score is highly effective for elevating myself over others. I'm convinced that I'm not correcting them to elevate myself—I'm simply acting in their best interest, stating the truth, and helping to make them better people. Of course, the fallacy of this thinking is revealed when others use this tool against me, and I feel shame and inferiority and react negatively toward them.

Scolding, criticizing, and finding fault are all about you. You know the right way, and things must be done your way. Oswald Chambers said, "Criticism makes you hard and vindictive and cruel, and leaves you with the flattering unction that you are a superior person."[1]

The more you trust in the personal sufficiency of Jesus, the less you need to scold, criticize, and find fault with others, because you have no need to be elevated above anyone else—you are fully accepted in Christ.

Tactic #6: Being Offended

Using this tactic teaches others to back off and cater to me or things will get difficult.

Closely related to keeping score, this is where I act hurt and misunderstood. It's so unfair what someone else thinks/says/does.

Being offended keeps me from hearing things I don't want to hear. It makes people treat me better, at least on the surface, because nobody likes to make someone else feel bad. It works incredibly well. Use this tactic enough and I'll also never get honesty from anyone.

Being offended is all about you and how you feel.

The more you trust in the personal sufficiency of Jesus, the less you need to manipulate others or act offended to feel better about yourself, because you have nothing to lose.

Tactic #7: Presuming You Understand

I use this tactic to judge a person or circumstance on the surface, in the first few moments, based on my own experience. I don't question that my experience might be incomplete or that there could be other dots to connect.

As a result, I come to incomplete or incorrect conclusions about others, but I treat them as if my conclusions are correct. And I never second-guess myself.

> We imagine we understand where the other person is, until God gives us a dose of the plague of our own hearts.
> Oswald Chambers[2]

You see this in news coverage every day. Stories are presented in simple headlines, often negatively. If all sides of a story are given, it won't be nearly as emotionally charged and entertaining.

The truth can be a lot of work. It's usually complicated and requires patience and grace. It challenges me to give the benefit of the doubt until all the facts are in. It's easier instead to select a few pieces of evidence that fit my agenda and then come to my own conclusions. I can stop paying attention since I don't need any more evidence. By the way, just like with the news, my conclusions are almost always negative and always make me look better.

Presuming you understand is all about you. You know enough to judge, and you're never wrong.

The more you trust in the personal sufficiency of Jesus, the less you need to judge others; you already have a judge, and he loves you and wants what's best for you.

———————

Wasn't this fun? See anyone you know?

Here's something far more pleasant: Let's say in a typical day you interact with family in some way a total of one hundred times. Just pretend it's one hundred. Let's say twenty-five of those interactions are expressions of one of the negative *Everyday Tactics of Family Disharmony.*

If you can swap just five of those everyday reactions for five of the reactions using the *Timeless Tools*, you've changed only 5 percent of your total reactions, but you've changed 20 percent of your negative reactions to positive, in favor of peace. You've made a major change with a minimal adjustment!

You're not adding anything when you begin adopting the *Timeless Tools*; you're simply replacing your negative reactions with positive ones. So let's begin to move out of the rocky rapids and into the more peaceful waters of your family river. Let's begin to rediscover the *Timeless Tools of Family Peace* and learn which ones the Lord might have you major in for your family.

Part 2

THE MOMENTUM-GATHERING RIVER

What can you do to promote world peace?
Go home and love your family.

Mother Teresa

— 5 —

The Peaceful River
The Timeless Tools of Family Peace

A harvest of righteousness is sown in peace by those
who make peace.

James 3:18

During my forty-year journey of discovering what makes families
happy—twenty years in rocky rapids and twenty years in peaceful waters—I've learned two things that are true about each of us
and that these two things are a big part of why we say what we
say and do what we do:

1. Everybody wants to feel good about themselves and look
   good to others.
2. Everybody desires grace, patience, and encouragement.

I've learned that the *Timeless Tools of Family Peace* are designed to take advantage of our drive to feel good and look good. Why? Because they're full of grace, patience, and encouragement. Every human being is designed to respond positively to their use. The *Timeless Tools* are good for everyone—those in your immediate family and your extended family.

> *Every human being is designed to respond positively to . . . the Timeless Tools.*

These are the tools that changed my life and the direction of my family. They're the answer to my long-ago question, "How can my family be happy?" These are the attitudes, expectations, perspectives, and actions I learned from my friend Harold that were lost to me for decades, so lost that when I discovered them they felt like the *"Lost" Tools of Family Peace*.

Why Are They "Lost"?

These tools are lost to the extent that we don't use them. Maybe we can nod our heads yes when we see or hear them, but we've forgotten or ignored them, not believing they'll accomplish what they're designed to do.

You can grab a few of the tools and jump right in, or you can explore how they all work together. Whatever method you choose, any tool you use will improve your most challenging family relationships, and the more tools you use, the better those relationships will be. Using them together builds momentum.

This list isn't definitive; you may know other tools. Just remember: it doesn't do any good to only know them; if they're not used, they're lost.

Of course, they all come from that ancient Book that's still alive today, the most popular book in the world—the Bible. Few people read it and even fewer people follow it. That is how the tools came to be lost.

Found

If you are one of those who reads and follows the Bible, the *Timeless Tools* will be very familiar to you. As your use of them increases, they will be rediscovered by you, just as they are being rediscovered by me and my family.

They are guaranteed to work. But because we are imperfect human beings, they may not solve all your relationship problems. They will, however, make things better, not worse. They're designed by God to accomplish his purposes for good, even in what we call problems.

Following are the tools I'm rediscovering, and I'd love for you to rediscover them along with me.

The *Timeless Tools of Family Peace*

Woo Their Hearts

There's the easy, everybody-does-it way that never seems to work: tell 'em what they're doing wrong. Then there's the harder, riskier way that takes longer but brings true satisfaction: woo their hearts.

Scolding and criticizing are family relational defaults for most of us. The mentality is "That's not right, here's how to do it." I may not say those words, but that's how it feels to others.

Wooing is an invitation that leaves people free to accept or reject what we're saying, offering, or suggesting. Wooing is the "could" to scolding's "should." Of course, there's a place for scolding and criticizing, but they are needed less often than I used to think.

The power of wooing is in its non-agenda, in the feeling it gives to others that, when I woo, I have nothing personally at stake in their response. It gives them permission to focus on what's in their best interest, not mine.

Wooing more and scolding less has been a fundamental shift in how I think and act. In a sense, all of the *Timeless Tools* add up to wooing. The more you use, the more you woo.

Get Your Peace Right

Everybody wants to feel good about themselves and look good to others. This desire is built into us. It's designed to push us to Jesus for our feel-good and look-good so that we experience his sufficiency for every need, want, problem, fear, disappointment, ambition, confusion, loss, comfort, emotion, and pain. We're designed to get our inner peace and affirmation from the sufficiency and love of Jesus. His sufficiency gives us a bottomless reservoir from which to serve and be generous.

> We are not to look to our family as the source of the inner peace and affirmation that only Jesus can give.

This idea is so important and radical that we'll spend an entire chapter exploring it a little later. For now, I'll summarize it this way: We are not to look to our family as the source of the inner peace and affirmation that only Jesus can give. We're not to need our family to treat us a certain way in order for us to be at peace.

This is the core of our usefulness and influence in our families. Needing certain reactions from your family leads to manipulation to get your needs met instead of being available to meet theirs. You can't meet their needs and your own at the same time. You have to choose.

Accept Your Family and Each Member Unconditionally

This is the opposite of PBA—performance-based acceptance from the *Everyday Tactics of Family Disharmony*. Acceptance says, "I love you no matter what. I accept you despite that thing you want to hide. You can't shock me or drive me away. I'm here to stay." Loving others unconditionally does not mean we love and accept all their conduct. Jesus did not condemn or reject the woman caught in adultery, but he did say, "Go and sin no more" (John 8:11 NLT). Acceptance of and grace for the real you from someone you love are powerful and liberating—you want that, right? That's what they want too.

Mixed emotions are natural. I'm to accept both my positive and negative feelings toward others. God does not go back and forth between loving and hating. He loves us all the time, even knowing all the negatives about us. I want to do that.

Each of my family members is an individual on their own personal journey and accountable to God. God is not finished yet, with them or with me. Our journey is tough enough without rejection and conditional love from the ones closest to us. Unconditional love is a miraculous human offering that goes deep into souls.

I want to accept my family as they are, not as I wish they were.

Accept Your Role and Your Limits

My role is to influence, not to dictate.

I've been placed in my family by God so that he can influence my family through me. Yes, they've got the same purpose of influence with me, but I control only me.

I'm limited in that I can't make anyone do anything, so I don't want to act like I can. Since I control only me, not them, I want to model more than tell—that's what Jesus did. I can take the initiative to influence for good no matter what anyone else does.

When we move in the direction of accepting our families unconditionally and in the direction of accepting our role to model what we want to see, we're walking with Jesus. This is his direction. He's with us.

So we want to take responsibility for our influence but free ourselves from responsibility for the results. We cannot control how others will respond to our influence.

Be Genuinely Curious and Attentive

When someone is genuinely interested in you, don't you feel honored? Curiosity is the opposite of indifference. When you feel accepted and honored, you calm down and your self-protective exterior softens. How does a calm, soft, unselfish family sound to you?

We want to listen with no agenda other than wanting to know and understand them. We all have a sixth sense that tells us if someone is truly interested or instead looking for evidence with which to judge us.

Genuine curiosity and attention convey the message that others are valuable and worth listening to and that we believe our curiosity will be satisfied by discovering something worthy about them. This causes people to feel honored, valued, and loved. And they relax. Then we can hear their heartbeat and learn what God is up to in their lives and catch a glimpse of God's vision for them.

We all love having someone who cares enough to commit to what God is doing in us, and your family would love to have someone like that too. Be the caring gift they long for.

Make Sure You Hear and Are Heard

Remember how it felt when you were a kid and one of your parents (or both) thought you were guilty of something you didn't do just because on the surface you looked guilty? And you said they just didn't understand? This tool is just the opposite. It's the reverse of one of the tools of disharmony.

I'm always tempted to assume I know what someone else is thinking or why they do what they do. I'm learning to own that I might be wrong. And I'm realizing they might not understand what *I* mean or why *I* do what I do. I have to own the responsibility to be clear.

It's natural and tempting to judge a person or circumstance in the first few moments, just from our own experiences. But let's always assume there's more to the story. While we may never know all of it, we can learn more than what's on the surface. We can gently take the initiative to converse, ask, listen, discover.

I want to make an effort to understand my family members, and I want them to understand me. There's an art to this, and this art is great training in patience and grace.

Embrace God's Vision for Them, Not Your Vision

It's easy to assume that my opinion of who someone should be and what they should do is right, but in reality, it's hard to even know what's best for my own self. If I'm going to embrace God's vision for others, then I need to have a clue of God's vision for them.

How do I get these clues of God's vision? It's a natural result of using certain other *Timeless Tools*. In the next chapter, "Contagious Momentum," we'll see how using a few of the tools together can multiply their effect. When I accept my family members, and I'm patient, curious, and attentive, I start to hear what God has put inside them. When I try to understand them, I go deeper into the sacred ground of God's vision for them.

I'll never see the entirety of God's vision for them, but I will see far more than my own surface assumptions of what's best for them. This helps me love them, makes them feel good, and honors God.

Be God's Access to Your Family

I want to let God reach my family through me. Needing my family to meet my needs to feel and look good blocks God's access through me.

You and I have been placed in our families for God to influence them through us. The influence is not so much ours as it is God's influence through our presence. Then we cooperate with what we see him doing in our families, which ties in with the previous tool of embracing God's vision.

When we're patient, curious, and attentive, we begin to see inside the soul of another and see what God is up to in that person. We learn who they are and how they feel and why they do what they do. We hear their heartbeat. We then have the awesome honor of cooperating with God in what he's doing in this person we love.

> You and I have been placed in our families for God to influence them through us.

Can you see yourself as God's hidden treasure in your family to influence those you love toward the things God has in mind? Even if you can't see exactly how to be God's access, can you accept that you are and that he's put you there on purpose to do good for them?

Encourage Six Times More

When someone gives you several compliments and then mentions something negative, maybe a correction or criticism, what do you go away thinking about? What do you follow up on? "Hey, thanks for the kind words, but let's go back to that 'could've been better' part. What did you mean by that?" Right?

No one ever says they get too much encouragement. There's an internal default in each of us that says receiving criticism weighs far more than receiving encouragement.

From the many things I've read, I've concluded we need to encourage five times more than we criticize or correct for the person to feel the encouragement is *equal* to the criticism. This means that when we encourage five times more often than we criticize, people still don't feel encouraged—it feels neutral to them. We need to encourage at least *six times* more often. When we feel we're going overboard with encouragement, we're probably getting closer.

We all have the secret superpower ability to energize and inspire through encouragement. It gives people much-needed confidence, helps them be all they can be, and connects them with us in ways good for our relationships.

Reject Passivity in Relationships and Situations

I'm naturally passive in regard to things requiring purposeful engagement. If it's a problem, a meeting, a phone call, a conversation, I'll put it off and hope someone else steps up to deal with it. Not everyone is like this, but I see many who are. We don't like to raise our hands.

This behavior is not good for family relationships. Avoiding issues tends to make things worse. They rarely get better on their own.

When people are left to sort things out for themselves, they almost always come to a negative conclusion. It's my job to take the initiative in my relationships and make sure I'm understood and give others every chance to be understood.

> *Avoiding issues tends to make things worse. They rarely get better on their own.*

I can't say, "You should have told me what you thought I meant." I need to take that first step and ask questions and ensure understanding. I'm not to just let things go. I'm to engage people and issues and handle them with grace, patience, and confidence. I'm to accept responsibility for my role of influence. This doesn't mean I confront; it means I am aware and sensitive to what is happening in my family.

Model What You Want to See

Modeling works better than telling, speechifying, or scolding, not only with attitudes and behavior but also with embracing the *Timeless Tools*.

Telling people what to do and how to do it is a default in most of us. It comes easily and naturally. Modeling requires humility and is more difficult—it's often tougher to actually have the right attitude or behave appropriately myself so others can see how it's done. If you're getting agitated and raising your voice, I can't just say, "You need to calm down." I need to be calm myself.

Jesus modeled how he wants us to live. Show family members what modeling looks like in your life and watch it become contagious.

Be a Safe Place to Launch and a Soft Place to Land

Family is most satisfying when it's a safe place to launch (with encouragement and rooting for each other) and a soft place to land (when learning to handle failure and disappointment without shame or condemnation).

Family is designed to be a place . . . where people know you best yet love you most.

Family is designed to be a place of honest vulnerability without rejection, disagreements without anger, foolish mistakes without embarrassment—the place where people know you best yet love you most.

I can control how I respond to situations out of my control. I don't have to make things worse. I can be an example of a soft attitude when offended or hurt. I can be unshockable and shockingly graceful. I can show that I believe this family place is safe by being vulnerable myself. Grace and vulnerability are contagious.

Don't Keep Score

As we discussed in chapter 4, no one keeps score of how many times they've been wrong or offended someone. They only keep score when others wrong them.

Since we like to keep score and we like to win, here's a radical score we could keep: *Whoever gives the most grace wins!* Turn around how you usually think of winning. I want to win at giving grace. To give grace, I will need to experience offenses and unfairness.

I can be a ruthless competitor in this. I can make sure I err on the side of too much grace and generosity to make sure I win. This is not just a game; I'm making a serious point.

I can never be taken advantage of if my goal is to out-give and be more generous than everyone else. If someone experiences unfairness, I have to fix it by making it fairer to them and less fair to me.

I want to trust that this one thing—humbly refusing to keep score—will kill the seed of bitterness and create a growing garden of grace in my family.

Be Unoffendable

If you're ignored, marginalized, or insulted, and you handle it as if nothing happened, you've just done something supernatural. In our world, people are supersensitive to their rights and easily offended. Remembering offenses in families is a main cause of division and pain.

For me, being unoffendable is only possible because I find my value and peace in the never-ending love and sufficiency of Jesus. When I get my feel-good and look-good from Jesus, I am secure. Therefore, I'm not easily offended when harmed or wronged.

This tool also ties in with accepting others with no PBA and with releasing everything to God. It's the opposite of tactic #6 of the *Everyday Tactics of Family Disharmony*.

Not being easily offended makes you easy to be around, easy to talk to, and easy to connect with. It also helps you to remain calm in challenging situations and to keep things from escalating. And it's contagious.

Do Things Together for Others

I've read that helping others, or volunteering, is one of the most practical things people can do that makes them happy. So it makes sense that if my family and I help others together, it can bond us closer together as we share the joy and experience of serving.

There's something about doing good for others that makes us feel better about ourselves and more valuable. When we do it together, it subtly works on relationships as well. Who has the inclination to disagree or get offended when we're in public doing good? If we can do this outdoors, it's even better—being outdoors is another thing that makes people happy. To be outside with my family as I help someone means that bonding and happiness are multiplied.

It's great to do anything together as a family, but helping someone together as a family—whether it's your entire family or only part of it—has the most beneficial effect.

Sprinkle Drops of Grace

Small touches add up. Words, actions, and favors send the message that people are loved and valued. When these small touches are unexpected and more than deserved, they create even more value.

I am confident that when I'm generous I am cooperating with and trusting a great law of creation that is built into humans: God has wired us to be sensitive to generosity so that we might be sensitive to *his* generosity to us in Christ.

Generosity is part of God's image, and he has stamped us with his image. The image is corrupted by the fall, and we're all now naturally selfish, but the seed and echo of generosity remain. You can water the seed with a little grace to get it to grow.

Little practical and thoughtful touches add up over time, and all those drops of grace create an environment for growth, which leads to more seeds and more growth. When I find ways to show my family that I'm their biggest fan, grace becomes contagious.

Release the Results, the Other Person, and Your Role and Limits into God's Hands

God loves more, cares more, and wants better for my family than I do. I'm realizing the great impact on others that comes from a peaceful attitude of trust. The burden of making things happen is on the Lord, but we have the privilege of cooperating with him and watching what he does.

He knows your family and you and your situation better than you do. He can do anything he wants, and he can be trusted to do what is right. Maintain a trusting attitude and watch peace spread.

Use a Mentor—for the Highest Use of the Tools

Everything I've been discussing so far has been influenced by a mentor. My mentor was Harold, but he preferred the term *discipler*. I use mentor only because I think it will be more familiar to you.

Before I met him, I didn't know the *Timeless Tools of Family Peace* existed. When I was first introduced to them, I didn't know how they worked, or why they worked, or which ones to use in various situations. But you've already seen through my story some of the difference a mentor can make in a person's life. Everybody needs help seeing and thinking. We all have blind spots. Often we need someone to simply affirm the importance and value of something

God has wired us to be sensitive to generosity so that we might be sensitive to his generosity to us in Christ.

we already know but are underestimating. One mentor for life is probably not the norm. Usually, we have several over the many seasons of life, each one helping with a certain season. They are invaluable and are a part of God's design for how he uses us in our families.

Obviously, these tools have not been handed down from on high on stone tablets. These are the ones that I have rediscovered and that contribute to the journey my family is on today. You probably have already thought of others that are contributing to your family's journey. But these tools are enough for us to see how God has designed our family relationships to work, and they're enough to keep us busy the rest of our lives.

And good news—these tools can build on each other, reinforce each other, and add up to an effect in your family far greater than you can imagine. That is what I call "contagious momentum."

— 6 —

Contagious Momentum
Our Families Are Designed
for Good to Spread

Everyone believes the world's greatest lie . . . that at
a certain point in our lives, we lose control of what's
happening to us, and our lives become controlled by
fate. That's the world's greatest lie.

Paulo Coelho

The day I "helped" my parents with their bills falsely taught me
that there's nothing we can do to change our circumstances. Their
resignation and shrug sunk into me as truth. I believed it for twenty
years. But it's a lie.

When I met Harold, I noticed a hopeful attitude behind everything he did. He always seemed to think if there was something
good that could be done, it should be done. He was not resigned to
anything being unchangeable or hopeless. This got my attention.

He convinced me I needed my first computer and then said, "Let's go to Best Buy now and get it." What? I wasn't used to the idea that I could decide to do something and then do it, all in the same day. This would be taking control of a piece of life, and I wasn't used to thinking that was possible.

You know why he wanted me to have a computer? Ministry. He believed it would help me to prepare and be useful in the lives of others. It would not be a toy, and it would not be just any tool. It would be a tool for a set purpose that he saw in me. He knew me and was trying to cooperate with what he saw God doing in my life. He had accepted me fully, I trusted him and opened up, he was curious and paid attention, and so he saw what God was up to. Now he was modeling the attitude and action he wanted to see in me.

I Was Discovering the *Timeless Tools*

Harold acts as if being purposeful and intentional is normal. But he's never controlling or pushy. He never tells me what to do. He mostly asks questions to help me think and come to my own conclusions. I never feel as though he has any personal stake in my following anything he says. He never calls me to check and make sure I'm on track. I think, *How can he just trust and not try to micromanage me? Don't you have to stand over people and make sure they do the right thing?* Harold doesn't do this, which teaches me something—he knows there's a God, and he knows it's not him. He's just a servant for God's purposes with me. He doesn't need me to need him; he gets his fulfillment somewhere else and always seems at peace no matter how things look.

I was with him in person one time per week, meeting at his home with a few others every Tuesday evening for years. Then for several more years I called him a few times each month with questions, mostly about how to live. He was always available, unoffendable, and forgiving of any potential offenses, such as when I went long periods without any contact with him. When I dropped the ball in a project, he'd say, "Let's call it a lesson and move on." Whenever he thought he needed to be tough, he'd back into it so gently that only later would I realize I'd been rebuked, like the time he called me a "spiritual masochist" because I seemed to refuse to allow God to bless me. I never walked away from a conversation with him without a tenfold boost in encouragement, a feeling that life is full of hope, and a belief that I had value and great abilities.

After a year or two of spending time with him, guess what I started doing? The same thing. In my family.

I began to hear his words coming from me, not mechanically but from a true embracing of his attitudes that I was adopting. I didn't try to be like him or practice or rehearse, but over time his influence was contagious and gained momentum with me. From me it spread to my family. Harold changed my family—and he's never met most of them.

It Takes Only One to Hear the Music

A man is sitting in a waiting room. He's subtly bobbing his head, tapping his foot, snapping his fingers.

Another man comes in and sits down. He notices the guy doing his rhythm thing, and after a few minutes *he* starts tapping *his* foot. Just slightly. Soon one of the fingers of his hand holding a magazine begins to tap the magazine.

Then the second guy realizes the first guy has earbuds. He's gettin' down to the beat. "Oh." The second guy is just copying the first. The second guy never hears the music.

Yes, you can follow the rhythm without hearing the music, as long as someone else hears the music and keeps beat with it. You can follow them, and you'll be in rhythm with each other and with the music, even if you don't hear it. In the same way, you can start the rhythm in your family.

Of course, it works best if you don't try to make someone else clap along with you. If you're just enjoying the rhythm yourself, and people feel as if you have no expectation of them joining in, it makes them want to join in more. We like to be free to want something on our own, don't we?

All it takes is one person hearing the music and enjoying it. So what is the music that others could clap to with you?

God doesn't say that the important things in life are to be smart and supertalented, or to be a winner or overachiever. Instead, what if the world we live in was dominated by people who are kind, tenderhearted, forgiving, patient, and humble, people who consistently say things that build other people up? That kind of world starts with that kind of family, and that kind of family can start with you. That's the music you could start clapping to.

The System Is Rigged in Your Favor

It's not surprising that, when I was growing up, I started out believing what I did because home is the most contagious place on earth. Families are wired for attitudes, expectations, perspectives, and actions to spread. Family is designed to be the easiest place to experience and learn love and grace. It's also the easiest place to learn dysfunction.

Families are wired for attitudes, expectations, perspectives, and actions to spread.

The opportunities to be offended and misunderstood are endless. The result of such offenses and misunderstandings is tension and bitterness. Parents, children, in-laws, grandparents—the entire family ends up living in this tension and bitterness.

But there's hope, because the opportunities for grace and love are also daily and endless. And there's hope because you can pick what you want others to "catch." When you *try* to influence for good, the contagious design of family automatically helps you.

Another reason for hope is that humans are created in God's image, with a built-in seed that longs to bear fruit that looks like God. We're wired to respond to encouragement and grace.

So as you adopt the *Timeless Tools of Family Peace*, you're taking advantage of the built-in cooperation of two designs: the design of family to be contagious and the design of your family members to respond to love and grace.

> *When you try to influence for good, the contagious design of family automatically helps you.*

The whole setup of family is waiting for you to set a beat that can be clapped to.

All Seeds Want to Grow

At first, changes in your attitude, behavior, and reactions may not be noticed. But when you create a mood or emotion that's pleasant and feels good, it begins to get attention and will be remembered. No one knows at first what it is or where it came from; they just know they feel good. That's the beginning, the seed.

When the new behaviors are repeated, your family starts noticing more and begins to connect the dots of feeling good with some words or behavior or person. Once they see the connection between feeling good and what seems to bring it about, things can start to grow. They can begin to seek it out. Where previously they felt bad in certain situations, now they begin to enjoy positive moods and emotions in these situations. As they take note of the settings or people that are related to the positive feelings, they start to want to be in that place or with that person. It feels good. Instead of avoiding you, they look forward to spending time with you.

<label>91</label>

Over time your family notices the simplicity of what's making them feel good: simple things you think, do, or say—or *don't* think, do, or say. Naturally, without trying, they mimic your behavior, simply out of the natural built-in contagiousness of family. They discover that it feels good to be on the *giving* end. They follow your lead, and not only with you but with others too. They begin to have the same effect on others that you had on them. And you're off.

Things just need to start. Your attitude and expectations can shift in a moment. The effect of that shift on your world is what takes time.

Your family and those in your most challenging family relationships may not have a clue about what the thing you all want looks like. And if they have a clue, they probably don't know what to do with it. Just like in my family, attitudes and behaviors in your family can be so habitual that change is barely a dream, and certainly not a hope.

We don't change attitudes and behaviors by printing out the Family Peace Polestar, passing it around, and saying, "Let's do this!"

They have to see grace, acceptance, and caring in action in everyday life, experience it, feel it—repeatedly—for them to see what might be possible and that it can become part of their world. The great news is that they're wired to recognize grace and acceptance when they see it and to respond to it positively.

Things just need to start. Your attitude and expectations can shift in a moment. The effect of that shift on your world is what takes time.

Here We Are

So far in this book we've explored how we feel about our family, about certain people, and about our hope for change. We've become sensitized to certain family members. We like the idea of family peace that we see in the polestar.

We're aware of specific attitudes—the *Everyday Tactics of Family Disharmony*—that have been causing trouble.

We're aware of the antidote to the *Everyday Tactics*—the attitudes, perspectives, and actions that get things going in a good direction through the *Timeless Tools of Family Peace*.

Now we're going to begin putting things together. We're going to see more of how the *Timeless Tools* look and feel for *you* in your family and in your most challenging family relationships. You'll begin to see how they feed and reinforce each other and how they can all work together.

The Unstoppable Small Beginning

At the top end of Lake Itasca, a small lake in northern Minnesota, a shallow flow of water maybe fifty feet wide tumbles out of the lake over a line of rocks. The rocks have long been a tourist attraction where people take photos of each other standing in the middle or crossing back and forth. Past the rocks the stream is about knee-deep and quickly narrows to about twenty feet wide, heads north, and meanders around the top part of Minnesota. Its course eventually arches down toward the Twin Cities, picks up width and momentum, then leaves St. Paul and heads south on the beginning of a twenty-five-hundred-mile journey to the Gulf of Mexico. Yes, this is the beginning of the Mississippi River.

> *We're each part of something God began, something unstoppable and picking up speed, something heading in a set direction.*

A few years ago a former Navy SEAL swam the length of the Mississippi River in honor of the families of fallen troops. Of course, he swam south, the direction of the flow of the river. You wouldn't want to swim against the current of the Mississippi, right? Same with the flow of our families. We're each part of something God began, something unstoppable and picking up speed, something heading in a set direction.

Cooperate with the Current

When Cademon and I paddled our canoe on the Rocky River, we were cooperating with an already-flowing current. The current provided the power to move us, while our paddling did the navigating and maneuvering within narrow limits of speed and direction. If we had laid our paddles across our knees and sat still, the canoe would have continued along with the current. The only way for us to stop our canoe was to pull it out of the water. Our paddling was for cooperating with the river and influencing our experience of the journey.

Canoeists learn certain paddling moves and techniques to navigate. Like the *Timeless Tools*, they have their own roles and names, such as boof, shuttle, creeking, draw stroke, sweep stroke, roll, and hip snap. A canoeist not only learns these paddling techniques but also learns how they work together to build momentum to help them navigate the river and current.

Working together and building momentum are exactly what happened in my family, and they can happen in yours. Gradually and consistently, Harold began paddling, and as things began to gain momentum, I joined in. Then Brenda and the kids joined, all of us learning together to maneuver and navigate as the current carried us. Then Myquillyn's and Emily's husbands Chad and John, and the families they came from, contributed to increased momentum. The canoe moved straighter and faster, and we learned to navigate with stability in a variety of challenging conditions.

When canoeists first begin to purposefully navigate the river, the biggest challenges are getting stable, learning when and how to use the different paddling techniques, and gaining confidence in changing conditions. Momentum builds imperceptibly. In the end, they become almost one with the river, reinforcing the momentum with selective techniques and maintaining it with minimal energy.

So too in our families. Over time everyone recognizes the tangible evidence of increasing grace and peace and feels the momentum growing.

The Design of Family Multiplies Your Efforts

Within a family, the design multiplies your efforts. God is on your side, or more accurately, you are on God's side and joining him in his plan and goal. If you start your part, the built-in design for contagiousness takes over. Plus, the built-in design of people to respond positively to love and grace helps them automatically drink in love and grace, like water soaks into soil: you don't have to make the soil receive water; you just water it.

The paddling required isn't physical energy or time. It's the "work" of sacrifice, selflessness, humility, putting others first, keeping your emotions in check. You don't do something more; you replace what you usually do—the attitudes and actions of the *Everyday Tactics of Family Disharmony*—with the attitudes and actions of the *Timeless Tools*. Only one person is needed to begin paddling, one person who takes the initiative. Gradual, consistent momentum will follow.

> *The built-in design of people to respond positively to love and grace helps them automatically drink in love and grace.*

There will still be problems, but they will dominate less and less. More and more, your family will feel like the family you long for, the family you see in the Family Peace Polestar. This is not meant to be some big undertaking. It's not your paddling that moves you downriver. You're in a current that's already moving. You're navigating, cooperating with the purpose of someone who created you and your family—do you think he might be with you in the middle of this? You have the purpose and design of family kicking in momentum to help you. And as a bonus, your family is already open to grace and love, and grace and love are contagious and will multiply.

Gathering Momentum

Remember the people who came to mind when you pictured your most challenging family relationships in the Family Satisfaction Assessment? Remember how you felt about your family relationships overall? In those challenging relationships, and in your family as a whole, let's look at where you're going by God's grace. This is what the process looks like and how the *Timeless Tools* affect and play off each other.

You are accepted and complete in Christ no matter what's going on in your family. Innately, you know that if your soul's not satisfied, you can't be who you need to be for your family. So by faith you say, "Jesus is sufficient for my built-in desire to feel good about myself and to look good to others," and you trust God to prove it. And he does.

When you find security and peace in the unchanging sufficiency of Jesus, suddenly you find yourself unoffendable, with no need to keep score (since you can't lose). You don't need to demand correct behavior before you can love. You find it easier to forgive and release bitterness, and you become a safe place to launch and a soft place for someone to crash-land. When others sense this confident trust in you, they'll be more open to your influence because your needs are no longer an issue.

Because you have found your own acceptance in a source outside of family, you accept your family—and every member—without reservation or expectation. You accept them as individuals because you love them, because family is supposed to be the place of acceptance, and because this is what Jesus does. Sure, you desire certain attitudes and behaviors from them, but you don't require a certain level of performance before accepting them. You accept your role to influence your family without pushing or scolding. You accept the limits of your influence and are at peace with the understanding that you can't control anyone or make them do anything.

Continuing Momentum

Your attitude of acceptance causes your family—even those in your most challenging relationships—to trust you more. They come to believe that you no longer have any secret agenda for them. They feel valued for who they are, not who you want them to be. They relax around you and let their guard down, allowing their true self to be revealed.

As family members open up to you, you're sincerely curious and find moments to give genuine attention, because you want to know what God is up to in each person. You care about them, and they feel it. You want to understand how they feel and why they do what they do. You're patient, and often your conversations involve you gently asking question after question, just out of curiosity. This causes them to trust you even more and to bond with you.

As they open up and you hear their heartbeat, you catch glimpses of what makes them tick and of what God is doing in them. Since this is God's work, you leave it to him to bring about what he desires. You get the privilege of cooperating with God and watching what he does. You embrace God's vision for them.

You see yourself as God's access to this person and to your family, and you want to cooperate with God in what he's doing with them. You find great fulfillment in encouraging them and helping them follow the path God seems to have laid out for them, not only in what they do but also in the kind of person they're becoming. You see how God has made each person unique, and you're confident that embracing their uniqueness is honoring to God and best for your family.

Contagious Momentum

You do your best to model what you want to see in them with no conditions, scolding and criticizing less and wooing more. You know that modeling the attitudes and actions of the *Timeless Tools* is highly contagious, and you're greatly encouraged as you see your attitudes and behavior catching on in your family and in your most challenging relationships.

All along, you continue to release your expectations for results into God's hands because you trust him. You release each person and your entire family to God, knowing that he loves and cares for them more than you do, and trusting that he knows what's best for them and you.

Your trust in God results in a growing patience with each person and with how things look. You lighten up. You recognize that everyone needs grace, patience, and encouragement and that everyone wants to feel good about themselves and look good to others. You resolve that for anyone who can't find those things in Jesus, they will find them in you. And you resolve that when they do find them in Jesus, you will reinforce them.

———

You've got the big picture. In the next few chapters, we'll take a closer look at some of our tools and learn how to navigate our family rivers the best way we can.

7

Get Your Peace Right

The Peace That Transcends All Understanding

When once we get intimate with Jesus we are never lonely, we never need sympathy, we can pour out all the time without being pathetic.

The saint who is intimate with Jesus will never leave impressions of himself, but only the impression that Jesus is having unhindered way, because the last abyss of his nature has been satisfied by Jesus.

The only impression left by such a life is that of the strong calm sanity that Our Lord gives to those who are intimate with Him.

Oswald Chambers

When we moved to Texas many years ago—the time when Harold told me to put away all my lists—the passenger seat floor of our Camry was piled with tissues soaked with my wife's tears. Leaving family and a new grandson and starting over again in a strange land with no friends brought Brenda to the end of herself. She had been on the way to the end of herself for a long time.

For years, next to her in bed in the dark, I lay on my back with my eyes open, praying through the ceiling, arms raised straight up in the air like I was a dead horse. *Lord, how long can she go on like this?* She was asleep and never knew.

Brenda lived an agitated, anxious life. You didn't usually notice on the surface, but the anxiety was always there inside like a distracting buzz.

In This World You Will Have Trouble

We all live with issues every day that are a potential source of anxiety: marriage, finances, children, work, friendships, expectations, health problems, self-esteem issues, desires, needs. These issues rotate, may be resolved, disappear for a while, and return. New issues enter the rotation and old ones dissipate. It's part of life.

For Brenda, her soul seemed to say, *I can't have peace until all that stuff is fixed.* Which is impossible.

Friends misunderstand you? No peace.

Pain or headache that lasts longer than a day? No peace.

Husband within twenty feet of another woman? No peace.

At every moment of every day for twenty-five years, one or more of these words applied to her: jealous, insecure, argumentative, anxious. The emotions were all under the surface but burst out in ways that confused a mere husband, though they were always mixed with a gentle personality. Gentle and agitated, that was her.

She was a sweetheart, and I loved her madly. Her suffering killed me.

One day I came home from work and she was reading a book. She held it out to me, pointed to a page, and said, "Is this true?" It was something about the finished work of Jesus Christ accomplished on the cross, not just for heaven but for here right now. Something like this: "In him the whole fullness of deity dwells bodily, and you have been filled in him" (Col. 2:9–10). She saw that she was complete, as filled with Jesus as she could be.

"Oh yeah, that's true."

That was the moment everything changed.

A supernatural peace was born in her. It was a silent, unspectacular turning point. She began to become a woman of grace, instinctively trusting the sufficiency of Jesus for everyday living. "It's the hardest, easiest thing you'll ever have to do," she says. "It was a trusting in verses such as 'My God will supply every need of yours according to his riches in glory in Christ Jesus' (Phil. 4:19) and 'I have been crucified with Christ. It is no longer I who live, but Christ who lives in me. And the life I now live in the flesh I live by faith in the Son of God, who loved me and gave himself for me' (Gal. 2:20)."

She had been a Christian for twenty-five years but still believed there was something left undone inside her, as if she was still incomplete. Then, God personally showed her, in a way I still don't understand, that all her "undones" were done on the cross with Jesus. And she believed it. "I was sharing his life. I wasn't on my own," she says. "Spiritually, it's not my life anymore; Jesus is alive in me living his life through me." You've probably heard people say this before. Brenda experienced it.

No circumstances changed. We lived in Texas for four more years. All the daily potential sources of anxiety remained. Yet peace and godliness reigned. Jealousy was gone. Insecurity and anxiety ceased to dominate. There seemed to be a deep well inside her more than sufficient to match any thirst, and she knew it. She experienced what John 4:14 says: "Whoever drinks the water I give them will never thirst" (NIV).

For me, it was too good to be true. Do you know how difficult it is to satisfy someone who needs you to be Jesus? This was after my initial discovery of the *Timeless Tools*, after Harold helped show me things that started making Brenda happy. I was already learning how to have a happy family, but the radical effect of peace in her had a radical effect on me. She took a giant step in peace and thereby took the pressure off *me*.

Her peace drew us closer. I didn't need to protect myself anymore from being misunderstood or wrongly accused. I didn't have to be afraid to be myself. Any reaction she was going to have toward me was not going to be based on any needs or agendas of hers. I didn't need to filter my words and actions through their potential to cause strong negative emotional responses from her.

When Brenda found that peace, she ceased to be so preoccupied with what the words or actions of others could mean. She still noticed what people said and did, and had an opinion about them, but their words and actions didn't affect her as much. She turned everybody loose to be themselves—not a perfect release, but far beyond what she had been able to do previously. For her, life became what James 3:18 promises: "A harvest of righteousness is sown in peace by those who make peace."

See what peace does for other people? That's the effect *your* peace can have in your family. And right now, I'll bet you are thinking of what someone else's peace could do for you, similar to what hers did for me. And it sounds good to you. But there's something better than that: it's what your own peace can do for yourself. As great as Brenda's peace is for me, it's nothing compared to what my own is for me. Unlike her, I can't describe the journey. I only know where I am today.

Once you experience the peace that Jesus gives, you won't want to settle for anything less.

The Trouble That Transforms

Unfortunately—you knew there was a catch, right?—peace often comes as a result of pressure. Before Brenda found peace, there were years of pressure. If you've experienced years of intense pressure in your family or in certain family relationships, you may be only a small shift in perspective away from real peace.

Peace doesn't *need* to come from pressure. Any of us can choose at any moment to believe and trust in the sufficiency of Jesus, but usually we need help, and the

Unfortunately . . . peace often comes as a result of pressure.

Lord knows exactly how to help us. The stress and pressure we feel from our most challenging family relationships are Jesus helping us right now.

Your peace might come in baby steps, like mine, or you might take one giant step in just a few moments, like Brenda. But chances are it will somehow come as a result of the pressure of problems.

Jesus wants me to truly experience his peace, not just give lip service: "My peace I give to you; not as the world gives do I give to you. Do not let your heart be troubled" (John 14:27 NASB). I think he's even *determined* for me to find my peace in him, and he'll never give up engineering my life to bring it about. I want to solve my problems. He wants me to give up trying to control and fix things myself and let him use the pressure of the problems to draw me to him for relief. It works. It's working now.

It worked when I tried to make Brenda happy and couldn't and was led instead to discover Jesus as the satisfaction I had been seeking from her all those years. It worked when I needed relief from regret over how I lied to Brenda for so long about my drinking. It worked in my disappointment over not being able to connect with my dad

> Come to me, all who labor and are heavy laden, and I will give you rest. Take my yoke upon you, and learn from me, for I am gentle and lowly in heart, and you will find rest for your souls. For my yoke is easy, and my burden is light.
>
> Matthew 11:28–30

before he died. It worked when we lost jobs and had to start over in new states five times in fifteen years. And it worked when we lost the last job at age sixty-three and decided not to pursue the next job and to instead buy a fixer-upper without a job or fixer-upper experience.

When I say it "worked," I mean the pressure of those situations forced me to seek my peace and sufficiency in Jesus. Of course he was doing other things in those changes as well. But I know he was also wanting to use those circumstances to increase my dependence on him: "Whoever abides in me and I in him, he it is that bears much fruit, for apart from me you can do nothing" (John 15:5). It worked.

During one of those times, I was driven to memorize some words from Hebrews 12. This isn't exact but is how I now quote them: "God disciplines us for our good that we may share in his holiness. Discipline produces a harvest of righteousness and peace in those who have been trained by it. So strengthen your feeble arms and weak knees." Notice that he says, "in those who have been trained by it." It's possible for me to experience problems and challenges and *not* be trained by them. Only if I allow God's discipline to train me do I get the righteousness and peace. And it's a harvest of righteousness and peace.

The Privilege of Unresolved Problems

King David often woke up in the middle of the night obsessed with thoughts of God. I have never lost sleep because I couldn't stop thinking of God. Yet even David, a man after God's own heart (Acts 13:22), did not do well in the good times.

He was much closer to God, more alive spiritually, when he ran for his life, needed rescuing, and lived with unresolved problems. When times were good, he disengaged from his kids, got lazy, had an affair, and then covered it up by killing the husband. Prosperity was his enemy. But the bigger his problems, the more intimate he was with God.

I want relief from challenging relationships. I want solutions and answers. I want things fixed. I want satisfaction and release from the tension between how things are and how I think they should be.

But I want these things more than God does. He could snap his fingers and fix everything, but since he doesn't, he must have other priorities for me. One of those priorities is for me to develop my personal relationship and intimacy with him. Like he did with Brenda.

He could snap his fingers and fix everything, but since he doesn't, he must have other priorities for me.

Unresolved problems are good for me and pleasing to God because they provide opportunities for me to personally experience his sufficiency and not just know it in my head. They must be a big deal because he so often creates or allows opportunities for me to find satisfaction in him alone.

Usually, however (and knowing better), I still try to find my greatest satisfaction in solved problems. But the peace that comes from solved problems is not the same peace that comes from God.

> Do not be anxious about anything, but in everything by prayer and supplication with thanksgiving let your requests be made known to God. And the peace of God, which surpasses all understanding, will guard your hearts and your minds in Christ Jesus. (Phil. 4:5–7)

Bad times are good ways to discover the sufficiency of God.

Expect Confrontation with Your Own Insufficiency

Like me, Bill saw firsthand the effect of getting peace from the right source. His wife had been sick for years. One day he came home and was surprised to see her working in the garden. "You'd better stop and go rest; you know what's going to happen." He knew she had very little energy. She said she felt fine.

She was fine. Her illness had left her. And something else happened. A peace beyond understanding was born in her.

Bill was awed by the supernatural change in his wife. He grew to want the same thing. He began praying that God would change his life too. He knew that the struggle and hopelessness of her illness were key to how God had changed her life, so he assumed it would be the same for him. In faith that God would answer his prayer, he made preparations at work and financially for a long incapacitation.

Bad times are good ways to discover the sufficiency of God.

Instead, his wife asked him for a divorce. Thus began his own dark night of the soul. He was forced to confront what kind of man he must be to cause his godly wife to want to divorce him. Like her, he was squeezed into unsolvable problems. Like her, he came out the other side into humility, grace, and peace.

They didn't divorce. Bill started going to a Bible study attended by hundreds—not at church but at work, inside a Fortune 500 aerospace company. Later, he mentored Harold—the Harold who mentored me. Through Harold my entire family has been shaped. If my family can be shaped by people they never met, how much more can your family be shaped by you? But, as with Bill and Brenda, the most powerful shaping comes just between you and God.

Expect to Go Down so Others Can Go Up

Jesus came to earth on a mission of selflessness. His Father had plans to rescue people and creation. Jesus was the plan. We know what Jesus went through to accomplish those purposes: suffering, rejection, death. But we get scared when he says things like, "Just as you sent me into the world, I am sending them into the world. And I give myself as a holy sacrifice for them so they can be made holy by your truth" (John 17:18–19 NLT).

Yikes. He's talking to his Father about me (and you). I'm sent on the same mission of selflessness. No, I'm not called to go through what he did, but I'm still put here for God's purposes, not mine.

That takes shaping. The shaping is not fun. If I could just see a straight arrow connecting the pain of shaping with the purpose for it, the shaping might be more bearable.

But my arrow can't be straight because all the stuff needed to make me usable for God's purposes is crooked, confusing, and painful. It can feel like death. "Unless a grain of wheat falls into the earth and dies, it remains alone; but if it dies, it bears much fruit" (John 12:24).

For the joy set before him, Jesus endured the cross (see Heb. 12:2). Part of his joy came from faith in the full sufficiency of his Father's love and purpose for him.

I'm willing for someone to take the long, mysterious, selfless journey to accomplish God's purposes for me. But am I willing to do the same for others? For my family? For the ones on the other side of my most challenging family relationships?

You're Here on Purpose

You are a created thing. You are unique. You didn't make yourself up. You are not your own idea.

Your Maker knows how he made you. He knows your strengths, your weaknesses, your pace, your abilities, your potential, your limits. Did you ever think that he made you that way on purpose?

He knows the level of your ability to deal with life depending on yourself (your natural ability) and depending on him (your supernatural ability). Did you ever think that perhaps he limited your natural ability so he could make up the difference?

Your life is being engineered. He engineered placing you in your family, with those parents and siblings, or without any of them. He engineered your schooling and friends and job and marriage, or the lack of them. He's overseen, or permitted, all your experiences and circumstances.

He created time, and how it moves, and how much there is. Weeks, days, hours, and minutes are the same for everyone. He knows what's available to you today for any moment, for any project, for your life. He knows every interruption and glitch. And if you are waiting for some answers, he knows how long you've been waiting.

He did not give the assignment based on your ability to accomplish it but based on his.

You have an assignment to be God's access to your family. He knows what that assignment means and why he gave it to you. He knows what's involved and what's needed to do it. He knows it's your assignment, and he gave it to you fully aware of your limitations and challenges. He did not give the assignment based on *your* ability to accomplish it but based on *his.*

And, oh yeah—he loves you more than you love yourself.

Why Does God Love You?

Does he love you because you're awesome and do great things? Does he love you because he's God and the Bible says "God is love," so he has no choice? And he sort of wishes he didn't have to?

When my friend Tony talks to people who follow Jesus but feel unlovable because they still mess up, he asks, "When God punished Jesus for your sin on the cross, did he hold back a little of his wrath and put it in his pocket so he could take it out and fling it at you the next time you messed up?"

God loves what he has created. That includes you and me. One of the first things he tells us in the Bible is that he created us in his image. Then he directs the very first people to be fruitful and multiply and exercise authority over their domain. This is part of his image, and it is your heritage.

Part of your domain is the family that your fruitfulness and multiplication have produced. You have a role of influence to fulfill in this domain. The influence is to be humble, gentle, patient, considering others more important than yourself, promoting love by covering over offenses, trusting the power of gentle words, and speaking only what is helpful for building others up according to their needs and for their good. It looks like love, joy, peace, patience, kindness, goodness, faithfulness, gentleness, and self-control.[1]

You were not made to live a frustrated, disappointed, offended, bitter, critical, survival-mode, disconnected, estranged family life. You were made for love, acceptance, grace, connection, generosity, and forgiveness. You have been specially wired and gifted to cover your specific assignment, your course on the river. Your family is your course on the river.

But you were made to do this in union with God, not on your own. When you aren't in union with him, you look for people to serve you rather than serving others. When you do it in union with God, you fulfill your unique family calling.

Do you know anyone else exactly like you? Do you know anyone with your combination of interests, experiences, fears, hopes, disappointments, passions, and friends, and who also orders your favorite Starbucks drink?

Hot dogs and pencils are cranked out on an assembly line. Not you. You're handmade and one-of-a-kind. It's personal. Own it.

If all the pieces of a puzzle were exactly the same, they wouldn't fit. You have to be you to fit. You fit what you were made for. You were made to fit in your unique family for their good, your good, and the good of the world influenced by your family now and in generations to come. You may not know it, believe it, feel it, or want it, but you're fitted for this. You can doubt it, reject it, and run from it, "but who are you, a human being, to talk back to God? Shall what is formed say to the one who formed it, 'Why did you make me like this?'" (Rom. 9:20 NIV).

Home Is the Place

I don't remember where I heard this, but it stuck with me: "Home is the place where family members go when they're tired of being nice to other people." If "nice" is an external thing that you carry, it eventually gets heavy and at some point you have to set it down.

You set it down at home.

I've thought of another one: "Home is the place where family members go when they need appreciation, love, acceptance, and encouragement." Or it should be, right? But no matter what, the appreciation and love and acceptance are never enough, are they?

Families seem to go one of two ways: family members somehow gain security and get filled up and from that deep well foster acceptance and love with each other; then they go out from that place and do the same with others. Or empty people go out and act loving and accepting, but it's all external. They get tired, go back to their families, and act like they really feel—empty—and then get angry because their cup doesn't get filled. It doesn't get filled because there's a crack in the cup that holds love inside us. But there's a patch for the crack:

> "My grace is sufficient for you, for my power is made perfect in weakness." Therefore I will boast all the more gladly of my weaknesses, so that the power of Christ may rest upon me. For the sake of Christ, then, I am content with weaknesses, insults, hardships, persecutions, and calamities. For when I am weak, then I am strong. (2 Cor. 12:8–10)

Earlier in this chapter, I mentioned that you may be only a small shift in perspective away from real peace. Maybe my Upside-Down R-Ator could be a piece of that perspective shift for you. It's a different way to look at the things that challenge and trouble us. This has changed the way I think of every family relationship and every problem I face. This is how I see things when I get my peace right.

The Upside-Down R-Ator

You think those particular challenging family relationships—with your spouse, kids, parents, in-laws, siblings—are a big problem that needs to be solved. What if they are actually something very different from that? What if they are actually opportunities—invitations— for you to become a person filled with grace, patience, forgiveness, love, and humility?

You know that's the kind of person God wants you to be, right? Well, that is also the kind of person who will survive the pressure you feel. And that's the kind of person God is going to use to influence those relationships and problems in your family. That's the kind of person who will influence your entire family for generations.

So, what if these challenging relationships or these family problems are actually a personal invitation to become that kind of person?

Do you want to just solve a problem, or do you want to accept an invitation to become the person you were meant to be, and want to be, with the relationships you want to have?

You have a choice. What do you want to do?

> *Let's stop using our families for something they were not intended to be for us so that we can be what we were intended to be for them.*

Let's stop expecting to get peace from our families. Let's stop using our families for something they were not intended to be for us so that we can be what we were intended to be for them. Let's live more for them and less *from* them.

This is the heart and soul of the gift of accepting our families and each member. It's the beginning of our ability to be patient and to be God's access to our families. It's the hinge on the door of grace into the room of wooing more and scolding less. Getting our peace right gets us out of the way and simultaneously puts us in place so that instead of a barrier we're a blessing.

— 8 —

Accept Your Family, Your Role, and Your Limits

It Begins with You

Many a blessing has been lost by Christians not believing it to be a blessing, because it did not come in the particular shape which they had conceived to be proper and right.

C. H. Spurgeon

"I'd be a horrible God." My daughter Emily said it. "I'd be mad at everyone all the time. Especially at people like me."

My wife, Brenda, agreed. "I'd be shaking people by the shoulders right and left. You'd walk down the street and see people shaking." Twenty-four hours a day, one big peoplequake, you and me included.

But God doesn't seem to be mad at everyone, and we don't see people shaking. Is he just holding back? Maybe he's really angry inside and is gritting his teeth to keep from showing it.

Or maybe one of the things that makes him God is the ability to be completely right all the time and yet patiently tolerant of people who seem so completely wrong. It takes supernatural strength not to do something that you have the power and justification to do.

But why be tolerant? And why not use your strength to do what you have every right and reason to do?

Love?

After a great time of shopping at thrift stores one summer day, Brenda and I headed home, but for some reason I was in a bad mood. I was short with her. Then, getting out of the car in a huff, I accidentally dropped a bag and broke a half dozen juice glasses she had been excited about purchasing. That snapped me out of my selfishness, and I felt awful. She didn't say a word. I went inside and tried to drown my idiocy in a nap. When I woke up, she had dinner ready. I apologized again, and she smiled. It was as if it took no effort at all for her not to be angry with me. It was weird. And very powerful. I didn't want to break more juice glasses. I wanted to love her back.

> Acceptance is . . .
> not license to act
> unacceptably;
> it's inspiration
> to give back the
> same generosity
> you receive.

That's what acceptance does. Acceptance is forgiveness and grace and love all rolled into one. It's not license to act *un*acceptably; it's inspiration to give back the same generosity you receive. I even wanted to give back *more* than the generosity she had given. I didn't tell myself to feel that way; it was as if I was already wired to respond that way.

The family member in your most challenging relationship is wired the same way.

What would my response have been if she had scolded, rebuked, and criticized me? She would have been absolutely justified. I deserved it. But my response would have been something like, "Oh yeah, well what about that time you . . . I said I was sorry! . . . Sure, I messed up, but nobody died for crying out loud. Why get so upset about it? They're just juice glasses . . ."

Right?

She accepted me, she accepted her role of influence, and she accepted the limits of her control. She couldn't change me or the situation, but she sure could influence both, and she did. She wasn't going to get her peace from juice glasses. She was passing on the same acceptance and peace she was already experiencing from God. It made me want to pass them on too.

Begin with You

First, let's remind ourselves that humans are designed to influence each other, especially in families. That's scary, because to be a positive influence you have to take responsibility for that influence, which is hard. But that's also good, because when you *do* take responsibility, the design will automatically help you. This takes the pressure off. You don't have to make anyone do anything.

When you take responsibility, you start with yourself, with accepting your family.

Here's what I mean by acceptance: you change your attitude. You think, *This situation doesn't have to change. My family members don't have to change. I may want change, but my happiness and contentment are not dependent on anyone or anything else changing.*

My daughter Myquillyn always says, "It doesn't have to be perfect to be beautiful." Your family doesn't have to be perfect to be beautiful. If it did, there would be no beautiful families.

You can accept your family as a whole and accept each individual member. You can accept the reality of who they are and

115

their imperfections. You can desire change, but you don't make your acceptance of them conditional on them meeting some criteria of yours.

You accept their personalities and accept how God has created them. That doesn't mean you approve of all their attitudes or conduct. It doesn't mean you don't talk to them about those behaviors.

It does mean you love them anyway. Our family has a mantra for this, first said by Brenda's sister Lillie about a family member who drove her nutty: "You can't hide her. You can't hate her. You can't kill her. You just gotta love her." Love them anyway.

> *Your family doesn't have to be perfect to be beautiful. If it did, there would be no beautiful families.*

Each is an individual on their own personal journey and accountable to God. God is not finished with them yet, or with you.

This journey is tough enough without rejection and conditional love from the ones closest to us. We all need and want acceptance and love.

This is the beginning of what Jesus did and does for us: "God demonstrates his own love for us in this: While we were still sinners, Christ died for us" (Rom. 5:8 NIV).

The hopes and dreams and goals of your family may be different from your own. You have control over only your desires and efforts. Would it be challenging to you to set a goal to lose thirty pounds? How much more challenging would it be if you set a goal for *someone else* to lose thirty pounds? And what if you made acceptance of them conditional on them losing the weight?

Now replace that goal with one such as being respectful, or employed, or sober. Or kind, or sensitive, or unoffended. Or that they stop thinking negatively, or stop marginalizing and rejecting you. And let's say you won't accept them until they change. How does that feel in your family? What if they hold back acceptance of you for their own reasons? "To be fully seen by somebody, and to be loved anyhow—this is a human offering that can border on the miraculous."[1] Accepting and loving your family is a miraculous human offering.

Acceptance Can Transform the Person Accepted

I cried while watching *Phantom of the Opera*. A male friend told me he did the same thing. We were both surprised; we bonded in discovering our secret. And we both cried for the same reason.

Near the end of the show, we began to connect the dots of why this guy is so mean and angry. He's a talented genius who's disfigured, who's never been loved, and who's grasping for love and acceptance to the point of eliminating anyone in his way.

When he gets alone with Christine, he lifts the mask hiding his ugliness to kiss her on the forehead. Despite his ugliness, she accepts him and kisses him back. Experiencing acceptance of his true self, he opens up even more, and we discover that he has never ever given or received a kiss, not even from his own mother. It's overwhelming to him, and it's overwhelming to us. Maybe men cry because we identify with hiding rejection and loneliness under a gruff exterior. Now we see the real Phantom. We see past his outward behavior and sympathize with how he got that way. Each of us—even your family nemesis—has a story of how we got where we are.

(Spoiler alert if you haven't seen *Phantom of the Opera*!) The Phantom experiences grace from Christine, and then he gives it back by rescuing his rival for her affections and letting them both go free. Acceptance has softened him and connected him with someone in a way he's never been connected before. (End spoiler alert.)

How can you see beyond the stereotypes and connect with your family members? Accepted people open their hearts up and are generous; hurting people close their hearts up and hurt others.

If you're confused or scared or feel insignificant, you might be short-tempered and selfish and act in ways that hurt others. If you feel unloved, you might be lonely and bitter and do unreasonable things to try to get love. Fill a family or a marriage with hurting people, and hurt will be multiplied.

But if your need for love and acceptance and approval is met, you can stop grasping desperately for it.

Acceptance Transcends Telling and Controlling

Christine didn't *tell* the Phantom he should be gracious. He caught it from her. She was his access to something he needed. In your family, you are God's access to something your family members need. You can influence them toward the things God has in mind—if you'll accept that role.

That role may seem daunting to you, but the burden is on him to bring about what he has planned. When you accept your role as God's access to your family, you have the privilege of cooperating with God and then watching what he does.

There is great power that comes from a peaceful attitude of trust. This is the beginning of contagious momentum. From our trust comes acceptance of others, and what follows are moments of genuine attention, curiosity, and love, which often reveal what God is up to in each family member. These are the first attitudes and acts of a person cooperating with God. This is the beginning of modeling for your family. These are things that become contagious. When you accept your role to model, you agree to take the initiative no matter what others do. The results are not up to you, only the role of modeling.

Do you want your family members to be more patient, kind, and respectful? Then you be patient, kind, and respectful. Leave the rest to God.

Do you want your family members to take less offense and be less argumentative? Then you take less offense and be less argumentative, and leave the rest to God.

Do you want your family members to root for each other and have a more positive attitude? You know what to do.

No, of course you can't do it all, and you won't do it all perfectly; you are growing too. But you *can* do something, and you must. Don't just say, "They won't listen! It won't do any good! Look how they treat me!"

Once you get your peace right, you have all you need to accept your family members no matter their response. This may be tough, but remember that their response is not your job. Your job is to model and be an example—imperfect though it will be—of what you know is good and right.

> *Thank God I'm not in control, because then I'd be responsible for the results.*

Pastor Andy Stanley says, "We are never responsible for filling anyone else's cup. Our responsibility is to empty ours."[2] And Jesus's responsibility is to fill your cup so that you can empty it for others. Do you think he wants to do that? When you keep your cup full, he can't refill it. There's no room for him.

Thank God I'm not in control, because then I'd be responsible for the results. Do you want to be responsible for the results in your family? With control comes responsibility. My hands are full enough with the responsibility for just myself. Right now, you can put your family, your role, and the results in God's hands and lighten up.

When you move in the direction of accepting your family members and loving them unconditionally, and accepting your role to model what you want to see, and accepting the limits of your control, you're walking with Jesus. This is his direction. He is with you.

And it's worth it, even if your family doesn't change!

Acceptance Disables the Scoreboard

Some friends recently told the story of family members who have been mad at each other for years. They made talking motions with their hands to describe how each person is always talking about the other, still angry. Each thinks the other is more wrong and has committed more offenses: "Yes, I've made mistakes, but they've done worse . . ." And they know this because they've kept score.

When I don't forgive, I put my hope for joy and peace into the hands of another person.

You've probably heard the saying, "Unforgiveness is like taking poison and hoping the other person gets sick." When I don't forgive, I put my hope for joy and peace into the hands of another person. It's all up to them—if they change, apologize, and make it right, then (maybe) I will too.

Where's the love and grace in that? It's just a business transaction.

It's hard to live a life of faith when your happiness and peace depend on someone else.

Offenses are the easiest, most tempting, most subtle things to keep score of. Keeping score is also one of the *Everyday Tactics of Family Disharmony*. It disables family relationships.

Think of the times when you feel offended. Whether the offense is big or small, you know the feeling—it's not fair, it's not right, you're hurt, you're neglected, you put up with more than they do, you're put out.

The natural reaction is to retaliate or just get away.

When I'm offended, I want to "leave"—emotionally or physically. And sometimes you do leave—maybe a church or job or relationship—even when you don't know whether the next thing will be better. The next thing might be worse. Doesn't matter; the offense was not logical, nor is the response.

Offenses are often hard to release because of a subtle appeal none of us want to admit. There can be something secretly sweet about being offended—a little self-justification and self-righteousness feel surprisingly nice, though we all deny it.

The bottom line is you harden toward the offender. The offender becomes almost an enemy. You may start by giving a cold shoulder or the silent treatment, then you cut the other off emotionally, hoping they'll surrender.

Without thinking, you assume that if you rack up enough offenses, then you have a license to reject the offender, to get out. Everyone has their threshold of how much they'll take. If yours is low, you're always starting over with jobs, churches, and friends, and your family life is dominated by challenging relationships.

If there was a pill to cure being offended, the whole world would change.

Praying for the person who's the source of the offense is one cure. It's hard to pray sincerely and be mad at someone. When I don't pray, it's because I enjoy that secret, self-righteous rush.

> To be a Christian means to forgive the inexcusable, because God has forgiven the inexcusable in you.
>
> C. S. Lewis[3]

There is another cure: get your peace right.

You don't have to take advantage of your right to be hurt. You can choose courage, humility, and selflessness. You can choose to let offenders remove their masks and accept what you see. You can choose to try to understand why they said or did something. You can choose to consider that maybe you got their motive wrong. Maybe you even misunderstood the whole thing. All this choosing takes work, though: "A brother offended is more unyielding than a strong city" (Prov. 18:19).

But the work can be worth it: "Whoever covers an offense seeks love" (Prov. 17:9) and "Good sense makes one slow to anger, and it is his glory to overlook an offense" (Prov. 19:11).

Acceptance Creates a Safe Place

I'll bet if the Phantom had internet, he would have been grateful for the postsecret.com website. Maybe he would have felt a little better if he could have shared his pain. It's one of the most popular blogs in the world. It posts anonymous confessions from people who send in postcards sharing things they've never told anyone. Not just secrets but confessions of fears, hopes, regrets, and desires. Some are funny. Some are frightening. Some are heartbreaking, embarrassing, painful, silly, and repulsive.

People also occasionally send objects that represent their secrets. The most common items are rings and razor blades. Heartbreak and shame. Here, you take it.

If you had a secret or hidden dilemma or embarrassment, and you felt the need to share, why wouldn't you just tell someone? Tell a friend or family member. Tell a pastor or accountability partner. Or why have any secrets at all?

Your life is filled with people willing to listen. And it's easy to get their undivided attention. Just say, "I have something I need to tell you, but you have to promise not to tell anyone." That'll get their attention. If not, start to tell them something and then stop and say, "Oh, never mind, I probably shouldn't say that." Use either of these methods, and they will be utterly curious and obsessed with hearing what you have to say. So what's the appeal of doing it publicly and anonymously?

And what's the appeal of reading the secrets and pain of people you'll never meet?

You keep quiet with people you know because opening the door to the real you is dangerous. Those who go through the door could be shocked at what they find. They could reject and shame you. You feel shame just thinking someone might reject you. And seeing what's inside could hurt people you care about.

Rejection and shame and hurting people are scary. Deep down you want to connect and be known. When you read the secrets of others, you don't feel so alone. You're reminded that everybody experiences some kind of pain, regret, heartbreak, confusion, and shame. You thank God you're not the only one. Yet, it's still hard to believe you're not alone. Nothing really helps until someone you love engages the real you that you're hiding.

Hiding is the short-term, easy way. You avoid the risk of rejection, shame, and embarrassment. And you avoid the risk of hurting or disappointing someone you love.

But you also avoid doing anything about the thing you're hiding. Since no one who matters knows, you leave things as they are (as long as you can stand the pain). You stay in the painful hiding place. This isn't good for you or anyone else.

What *is* good for people is to somehow hear and experience this message: "I love you no matter what. I accept you despite that thing you want to hide. You can't shock me or drive me away. I'm here to stay." Then the dangerous place transforms into a safe place.

The safest place on earth is not the PostSecret website. It may feel safe, but it's a neutered safety. You won't experience judgment and rejection there, but you also won't receive the true love and acceptance you're hungry for.

Your Family Is Designed to Be the Safest Place on Earth

Yes, family can be the scariest place: rejection from a stranger is easier to take than rejection from someone you love. But it can also be the most awesome place: acceptance and grace for the real you from someone you love is powerful and liberating.

Your family is designed to be a place of honest vulnerability without rejection. Disagreements without anger. Foolish mistakes without embarrassment. Failure without shame.

> *For you and for those you love, your family is designed to be the safest place on earth.*

The place where they know you best yet love you most. An encouraging place to launch and a soft place to land.

If you feel your family is far from a safe place, how can you get there?

You can make your corner safe. Be unshockable, but be shockingly graceful. Show that you believe this family place is safe by being vulnerable yourself. Grace and vulnerability are contagious.

> Relationships don't thrive because the guilty are punished but because the innocent are merciful.
>
> Max Lucado[4]

For you and for those you love, your family is designed to be the safest place on earth. Commit to cooperate in your corner with the One who designed family that way, and he'll move heaven and earth to help you experience that safety.

Once people sense safety and do as the Phantom did—remove their masks and open up—all you need to do is the easiest, most natural thing: just listen! Pay attention, be patient, and follow your normal, caring curiosity. You're about to discover surprisingly deep connections.

— 9 —

Be Patient, Curious, and Attentive

Be the Caring Gift They Long For

I want to suggest . . . a tool that is practically infallible, almost always reliable, and surprisingly practical. A tool that not only helps you understand other people but simultaneously improves your relationships with them and helps you learn, in real time, how to communicate with them, even in—especially in—the face of conflict or disagreement.

That tool? Curiosity.

Peter Bregman

One of my jobs on the radio used to be talking to singers who came through our town. I enjoyed asking questions and listening and then asking follow-up questions. I was genuinely curious about what made them tick, so I naturally would probe a bit to discover who they were and why they did what they did. Sometimes people complimented me on my interviews.

One day a guest artist turned the tables on me. After we talked, she leaned over, put her elbow down on the counter, cupped her chin in her hand, and said, "So, what's going on in your world right now?" Then she smiled and stared as if she actually expected an answer. She meant it. This had never happened before. It was disarming. And it felt good.

My friend JJ does the same thing. He asks a question, shuts up and listens, then asks another question based on what he heard. Imagine that. It's as if he really cares.

A service tech guy visited yesterday to examine our crawl space. I came out of "The Monk House," my outdoor writing shed, and he asked what I do in there. "I'm writing a book," I said.

"Oh, what's it about?" he asked, and then he looked me directly in the eyes and listened intently. He was paying such close attention that it made me nervous and I stammered. I wanted to talk so bad I got tangled up.

And I've talked about Harold—he's the most intense listener I've ever been around. Even on the phone I get self-conscious, feeling his undivided attention even during my pauses. I'm sure he hears what I'm thinking. I want to talk, but it's intimidating. He also makes me feel valuable.

When someone seems genuinely interested in what you have to say, do you talk more? It works that way for me, and it makes me feel that there must be something of value in what I'm saying. When people talk more, we get to know them better.

Things Are Beginning to Add Up

So here we are journeying down the momentum-gathering river. You start with getting your peace from the One who *is* peace, and you release your family from any responsibility for your peace.

Then you do a tough internal thing: you accept your family unconditionally and accept your role to influence them on purpose. Hmm,
even without them accepting the same thing? It's tough, but yes.

What's next? Something you can do a little bit of every single day.
It's what JJ, and the singer, and the crawl space guy, and Harold did.

Let's say you and I are talking. I look you in the eye and sincerely ask a few insightful questions about
something you did, why you did it, how it
made you feel, and what you wanted to see
happen. I listen and ask a question and listen some more. You do most of the talking.

You can tell whether my questions and
curiosity are driven by duty, or my own self-
interest, or to catch you at something, or to
gather gossip. You can tell if I'm trying to
get credit for seeming interested.

And you can also tell if I'm curious
because I really am interested in you, and
because I think my curiosity is going to be
satisfied by discovering something valuable
about you. When someone does this with me, I feel honored. I feel
they care. I feel I must be valuable. And I remember who it was
that made me feel that way.

> *Be curious and
> sincerely care; listen
> without pushing or
> having an agenda.
> Do these things
> consistently in the
> little moments,
> and your family
> will feel honored
> and valuable too.*

Be curious and sincerely care; listen without pushing or having
an agenda. Do these things consistently in the little moments, and
your family will feel honored and valuable too. They'll feel loved.
And they'll remember who made them feel that way.

Curiosity + Attention = Love

When you feel honored, valued, and loved, what happens? You
calm down. Your self-protective exterior gets soft. You lose the
urgency to win and prove yourself and be right. You feel a bit

generous and unselfish. This is the same effect that comes from acceptance; you're reinforcing it.

How does a calm, soft, generous, unselfish family sound to you? Genuine curiosity and attentiveness move you in that direction, moment by moment.

Most of the time you don't sit down with family members and give each other undivided attention in a conversation. It's a good idea, and you look for opportunities to do so, but family life is usually as-you-go. But many little moments add up.

What do your attention and curiosity lead you to discover? What do you see when your curiosity is satisfied?

You see inside a person's soul. You learn who they are and how they feel and why they do and think what they do. You hear their heartbeat. You catch a glimpse of God's vision for them.

Curiosity + Attention = Vision

God's vision is not *your* vision for that person. It's a vision that's already present apart from you. You can't see the whole thing, but you get hints of it from the heartbeat that you hear in their soul. You get a clue that something is going on, and if you stay curious and attentive, you begin to gather dots to connect.

This is a privileged place. God is up to something in this person that he created, and you're getting a little peek at what he's up to. When this person is a family member and you love them, an awesome honor presents itself: the honor of cooperating with God in what he's doing in someone you love.

Here's where the ground can get shaky. You don't know everything that's going on, and you can easily mix in your own ideas and desires with what you think you see. This cooperation needs to be done with humility, since we hardly know what God is up to even in our own selves: "A man's steps are from the LORD; how then can man understand his way?" (Prov. 20:24).

We all need help understanding our way. Wouldn't you love to have someone who cared enough to commit to cooperating with what God is doing in you? Your family would love to have the same thing—and they do: you.

They're Already Revealing Their Heart

The caring and the cooperating begin with simply being curious and attentive as you go through the day. Even outside of a back-and-forth conversation, you can quickly learn about a person by listening to what they talk about unprompted, spontaneously. You may learn what really drives them or what they're passionate about.

Sometimes you learn more than they intend. The other day, in less than three minutes, I learned that the fellow next to me on the plane had two master's degrees, was pursuing a PhD, had never walked the aisle to graduate because he felt it a useless ceremony, was not paid what he was worth, and knew how the department he was part of should be run and had told his supervisor, who liked his ideas and was going to act on them "maybe next year." Do you hear his heartbeat? I learned all that about him without asking. In three minutes.

Other times I've learned about people going to Harvard or traveling the world or working with Chuck Colson or being a doctor and missionary for twenty-five years—all in the first few sentences without even asking. Sometimes the information comes out in the course of a conversation; at other times it's given right up front. At those times, perhaps individuals have a need to impress a stranger, in which case, if it's true, there's another thing you've learned by letting them talk spontaneously. Beat, beat, beat. And you heard their heartbeat just by being patient and paying attention.

The other extreme is the person who doesn't talk at all unless pressed. At a graduation get-together, a man walked in with his wife and didn't say anything to anyone. I watched him move around the room alone, without speaking, and finally go outside on the deck. I followed him and learned he's a lifelong farmer; had inherited the farm from his dad but it's OK if his own kids don't do the same, he'll just sell it; has never lived outside that county; married a woman from out of state; and has no desire to live anywhere else. He said that in the first two or three minutes, but only because he was asked questions. Can you hear his heartbeat? Listening to our loved ones speak spontaneously helps us hear their hearts unfiltered. You can then honor them with curiosity and attention by asking a few sincere questions about why they did that, thought that, said that. As they're forced to think about what they're doing and why, and how the little confusing stuff fits together, listen to their answers. Help them hear what they're saying. Only they know their situation and purposes and desires and everything they're considering. Sometimes you end up repeating their answers back to them when it seems they don't realize that they just said something meaningful or profound. Sometimes that thing becomes one little piece that connects other pieces together for them, and you see a little light go on. "The purposes of a man's heart are deep waters, but a man of understanding draws them out" (Prov. 20:5).

> *Listening to our loved ones speak spontaneously helps us hear their hearts unfiltered.*

You don't have to give advice, just help them hear what they're saying. We all need help realizing what we already know. A nice side benefit is that even when you don't tell them anything, they associate their enlightenment with your presence and may think you're a genius, which is OK too and helps them trust you more.

Major on Listening to Real Words, Not the Ones in Your Head

I regularly catch myself in imaginary conversations. Almost always it's when I'm trying to understand where someone is coming from, or I'm trying to convince someone of something that I think they just don't get.

I think that's normal, part of our effort to understand and sort things out. It's like sifting to separate the big rocks from the little rocks and the sand. It takes time. But we can go too far with this, especially with our most challenging family relationships.

When I find myself repeating the same things over and over in my head, having the same conversation, making the same arguments, I know I'm crossing over to the dark side—the dark side of control.

If I just think hard enough, talk to myself enough, work hard enough, I'll be able to make this thing I'm dealing with turn out the way I think it should. I'll understand. They'll understand. And I'll have peace. Baloney.

These faux conversations are useful up to a point. They help you gain some perspective and insight, and they help you rehearse a real conversation. All good.

The problem is it's *not* a real conversation. It's all just you. You're imagining what the other person is thinking and saying, and if the person is a family nemesis of yours, almost everything you're imagining them thinking and

> Criticism makes you hard and vindictive and cruel, and leaves you with the flattering unction that you are a superior person. There is always one fact more in every man's case about which we know nothing.
>
> Oswald Chambers[1]

saying is negative. Then you're responding to the negativity in your own head. You're making it up! You don't really know! You're arguing with yourself! What you are doing is subtly transferring trust for the results away from God and to your own powers of logic and persuasion. Which aren't much.

When that conversation in your head starts repeating itself and you feel anger building up, that's the sign to stop. I've had to tell myself to stop several times in the span of a few minutes. Those imaginary conversations lead me to conclusions about what someone else thinks and feels based on negative things I've invented. Then I treat them the way I would if the stuff I made up were true. Then I wonder why they seem bugged by me. So then I add more stuff to what I think about them based on their response to my negative false assumptions of them. And round we go for years.

I need to get out of imaginary conversations . . . and listen to the real *voice of the person I consider my nemesis.*

I need to get out of imaginary conversations and get into real ones and listen to the *real* voice of the person I consider my nemesis. My real conversations are almost always more positive than my pretend ones.

If you have a history of arguing in your head with someone, you can count on two things:

1. They're probably arguing in their head with you too.
2. The longer it goes on, the less chance either of you is dealing with reality.

Someone needs to stop the cycle of negative assumptions. I know from experience how challenging this is. Controlling your thinking is hard work. It's totally doable through God's help, but most of us don't make the effort. It's a rare heroic work of sacrificial love.

We build statues to mighty conquerors. But God says those who are slow to anger, with their emotions and thinking under control, are to be admired more than the person honored with a statue: "Whoever is slow to anger is better than the mighty, and he who rules his spirit than he who takes a city" (Prov. 16:32).

Controlling what you think of someone else is worthy of more respect than any notable achievement. Control your thinking, and a statue in your likeness will be built in your family legacy.

Finally, brothers, whatever is true, whatever is honorable, whatever is just, whatever is pure, whatever is lovely, whatever is commendable, if there is any excellence, if there is anything worthy of praise, think about these things. (Phil. 4:8)

Everybody's Got a Story—and No Matter How Well You Know That Person, There's More

I'm still getting to know Brenda. We've been married forty-three years as I write this. Recently, she said, "When I was a kid, I used to keep poems and songs in a black garbage bag." Nuggets of her heart and soul in a garbage bag. She wonders what happened to the bag. What does it mean that she kept poems in a garbage bag? Is it sad? Funny? She doesn't even know. It makes me wish that I could have been a grown-up or a big brother back then who could have acknowledged the value of her heart and soul, so I wouldn't have to wonder whether she knew it was valuable or just garbage.

> *Controlling your thinking is . . . a rare heroic work of sacrificial love.*

A couple of years ago we went back to Indiana to visit. While crossing the Ohio River in Louisville, Brenda told a story of their car breaking down near the river when she was a kid, how they all walked through a field to find help and a farmer gave them water in pop bottles to take back to the car to drink as they waited for help to arrive.

Forty years of marriage and I'm still hearing new stories.

After our daughter Emily grew up, we learned that the annual replay of *The Wizard of Oz* on TV was like Christmas to her. Her whole day at school would be filled with stressed-out excitement and anticipation. As much as we loved and knew her, we didn't get to be a part of it because we didn't have a clue about the thrill her heart was experiencing. I wish we could have shared her joy, made it a big deal, and celebrated with her. As parents, there will always be kid stories we know nothing about, but we'd like to keep them as few as possible, so we can have input into how our children interpret things at the time.

One day our daughter Myquillyn casually mentioned the year she bought all gray clothes for back to school. She said it wasn't on purpose, but it made her feel so complete because she had outfits that matched. And that reminded her of another incident. She was getting out of the car with her friend and needed a little money. Brenda didn't have her purse but told Myquillyn, "Honey, if I had five dollars I'd give it to you," and Myquillyn felt good because her mom would give her five whole dollars?! Those stories had happened more than twenty years earlier, but that's the first time I heard either of them.

Recently, out of the blue, one of Emily's high school coaches reconnected with her old team. She wanted to tell the girls what was going on in her life during those great days of fun and going to nationals.

What was going on was not fun. It was a time of severe challenges in some family relationships. She shared some details of those challenges. But, she said, God used her time coaching to encourage her and that the time with her girls was the highlight of her day. Of course, she couldn't share that back then. But now, over fifteen years later, she wanted the girls to know.

Emily said, "We never suspected. She really was a real person, not just a coach." She paused and then added, "No matter who it is, everybody's got a story."

When You Hear Their Story, You See Who They Are

I met a gap-toothed truck driver backstage at a concert a few years ago. I got along great with guys like him in my days building Cummins diesel engines. He laughed and talked joyfully about experiencing God's grace while driving through a snowstorm. A friend told me, "That guy used to be bad on drugs. And he drove for Elvis. And, oh yeah, his mom wrote 'Love Me Tender.'" Everybody's got a story.

I met another guy at the same concert—tall and skinny, one of dozens of nameless non-star band members. But everybody's got a story. He used to weigh over three hundred pounds. Lost one hundred fifty. But he refused to buy new clothes while he was losing weight. His waist had been fifty inches, and as he lost pounds, he continued to wear the same size pants, pinching them tighter and tighter, until he got down to the goal of his old high school weight. When he finally got there, his waist size was thirty-one inches. *Then* he bought new clothes. Why'd he keep wearing the too-big pants? Motivation—it kept him going. Can you hear his heartbeat?

The worst? My sister Alyson was sexually abused during a Fourth of July celebration at my dad's company picnic. It was decades before I knew. She didn't tell anyone. Our family didn't have the kinds of relationships in which she felt safe sharing. Even if we had noticed a change in her behavior afterward, we wouldn't have known what to say. Heartbreaking. It influenced everything in her journey of becoming, and she was all alone with it.

Multiply these stories times every person in your family.

It's easy to see people—especially a family nemesis—as one-dimensional and to forget that everyone has a story. Leadership consultant Peter Bregman says:

> As soon as we label something, our curiosity about that thing diminishes. . . . And once we know something, we're no longer curious. But that's not nearly as powerful as living in the mindset of "I don't know." True understanding comes from not knowing. Real connection comes from not knowing. . . .
>
> See people. Don't label them. Allow yourself to be surprised.[2]

When you hear others' stories, they instantly become as real as you. When they become as real as you, you begin treating them as you want to be treated, and your relationship is transformed.

There are two surefire ways to hear everybody's story and increase the chance of connecting and seeing what God is up to in their lives:

1. Listen. And if you listen but don't hear anything, then
2. Ask. And after you ask, do #1 again.

There's no such thing as a nobody. There is no nameless, faceless crowd, especially in families.

When you hear these stories, they become a permanent part of who these people are to you, and you gain some understanding of why they do what they do. When these stories are missing, part of who they are is invisible, and the way you relate to each other is incomplete.

Ask While You Can

Patience, curiosity, and attentiveness are not strategies but acts of love.

Tommy was my brother-in-law. He died about thirty years ago. He was a gentle, generous man to my wife, the little sister of his wife. Tommy was a car salesman all the years I knew him. I had heard he was a boxer earlier in his life, but I never asked him about it. I guess it wasn't interesting to me at the time. I had my own stuff going on with kids, unemployment, and too much beer.

Recently, we had a big family get-together, and Tommy's wife and daughters were there. As we were leaving, they brought out a scrapbook the girls created for their mom. It was filled with clippings, stories, and photos of Tommy's boxing career, including photos with Jack Dempsey. Tommy was a little guy, a Golden Gloves amateur. He lost only four of his first thirty-six fights. He won the California State Featherweight title. He fought in Madison Square Garden, Boston Garden, and the Cotton Bowl. His family has a gold badge giving them lifetime admission to any Golden Gloves event.

I never knew.

I'd love to ask Tommy about that fight with Ricardo Moreno. It was Moreno's first fight in America, and six thousand of his fans from Mexico filled the stadium. Another two thousand were turned away. What was that like, to have everyone booing you and rooting against you, screaming for the other guy to clobber you? What was it like in the dressing room after you lost?

And when you were knocked out in the first round of your last fight, did you know at the time it was your last? Why'd you retire? You were only twenty-four.

I'll never know.

You don't have forever to ask questions, to be curious, to care. Things change fast, and death is permanent. Your chance to make a firsthand connection with your family member's heart, life, and story evaporates. Instead of a flesh-and-blood, eyeball-to-eyeball encounter with a scene from your family movie, you get to stare at flat yellow clippings in a scrapbook. If there is a scrapbook. Your loss, and your family's loss.

> Let every person be quick to hear, slow to speak, slow to anger.
>
> James 1:19

You and your family's *gain* is that when you do hear that heartbeat and catch a glimpse of what God is up to, you have an opportunity to cooperate. Hearing a person's heartbeat draws you closer to God and closer to that person. If you're willing, you have the privilege of being one of God's accesses to that person, in the wonderful, personal, eternal work he has in mind for them and for you.

— 10 —

Be God's Access

You're God's Hidden Treasure
in Your Family

> The role of the director is to create a space where the
> actors and actresses can become more than they've
> ever been before, more than they've dreamed of being.
>
> Robert Altman

It was an experiment. The grandkids were dabbling at dinner,
and I wondered if they were going to finish. So I tried something.

Firmly and enthusiastically I said, "I can't believe how great
you guys are eating! Look at you!" I wasn't lying—I was giving
them credit for what I knew was coming.

They smiled. Then each one grabbed their fork to take another
bite.

I held a spoon to my mouth like a microphone and started
announcing loudly in a fake, macho announcer guy voice, "What

an incredible performance we're witnessing tonight! Never before seen in the annals of eating!'"

They laughed and ate some more. I kept egging them on, and they kept eating. Every bite became an amazing achievement, another milestone. Our time together was positive and fun, and they felt like they were accomplishing something. Five minutes later, they were done, clean plates all around.

I didn't tell them to eat. I didn't talk about what they should do. I didn't scold or make them do anything. But I was part of the change that comes simply from cooperating with how we are all created to respond to acceptance and encouragement.

The Hidden Treasure in Your Family

There's a hidden treasure buried in your family. That treasure provides your family with access to God's acceptance and encouragement and is uniquely created by him and divinely placed for your family.

Here's how to find it:

1. Walk into your bathroom.
2. Look in the mirror.

Your family's hidden treasure is you. Well, actually, the treasure is your *presence* in your family. There's a subtle difference between you and your presence. Your presence is God's access to your family.

On our own, we've proven to be feeble change agents in our families, wouldn't you say? What good have you brought about by the power of your will and personality and wisdom alone? For me, not much.

But God's presence through us goes to places we can't touch, places we don't even know exist. Yes, he can go there without us. But he created families as a place for us to influence each other while cooperating with him.

There's you. There's your family. And there's you *in* your family. None of that is accidental.

We love it when someone cares enough to commit to cooperate with what God is up to in us. Your family would love to have the same thing—and they do: you.

When you accept someone for who they are, when you're patient and curious, and when you give them the incredible gift of attention, that's when you begin to see inside their soul and see what God is up to in them. You learn who they are, how they feel, and why they do what they do. You hear their heartbeat. You then have the awesome honor of cooperating with God in what he's doing in this person you love.

I know what you might be thinking right about now, because I think it too: *Aren't there some other big, strong grown-ups in this family who also should model and cooperate with God?* Oh yes, but right now it starts with you. And you're enough to start with.

Maybe you've heard of Compassion International—they help match children living in poverty around the world with sponsors who enable the kids to get schooling and have their basic physical, emotional, and spiritual needs met. Where Compassion goes, whole communities are changed. Compassion president emeritus Wess Stafford says:

> While changed circumstances sometimes change people, changed people always change circumstances.
>
> One changed child eventually changes a family. A changed family will influence change in its church. Enough changed churches will transform a community. Changed communities change regions.
>
> Changed regions will in time change entire nations.[1]

Do you believe that? Because if big changes in a family can start with one small child, what kind of changes can start with one big, strong grown-up actively cooperating with God?

Be Up to What God Is Up To

Don't default to the common, "Well, I tried, and they just won't change" or "Things can't change because _____ _____" (fill in the blank with your favorite reason). You're better than that. God is bigger than that. You just haven't seen how it will happen yet. Don't give up.

The Bible says in Christ "are hidden all the treasures of wisdom and knowledge" (Col. 2:3). It also says the hope of glory is Christ in you (Col. 1:27). So if you're a believer in Jesus, and he is in you, where are those treasures? In you. And where are you? In your family. That person in your bathroom mirror is God's access to your family to influence them toward the things he has in mind. As we've said, since the things are in his mind, the burden is on him to make them happen, and the privilege of cooperating is ours. If you want to be God's access to your family, be up to what he is up to in your family's life.

God made each of our family members unique without asking our opinion, and he's going his own direction with each of them. For me to go with my agenda for who someone else should be or what they should do would be taking over God's job. No fun. I'd be fighting God. He may not be asking my input for what he's up to in my family, but he sure is inviting me to be part of it. I get to cooperate if I want to.

Here is the fun part: when I see a little of what he's up to in a family member, I take it seriously and see myself as God's agent or ambassador. If I'm acting in God's interests for the good of that person, I get to model and be an example of what I see God is up to. Instead of deciding what I want to see in another's life, and pushing, pointing, scolding, and correcting, I try to cooperate and model a bit of what God desires and trust that it will be contagious.

With kids, I may see interests in dance, cheer, skateboarding, hockey, or the like. If their interests change, do I allow them to move on, and move on with them, or do I resist because I've begun to take ownership of them as a cheerleader or hockey goalie? Latching on to my own expectations for someone can be sneaky easy. I can do the same with adult family members, having my own expectations for how they should behave or what they should do. This prevents me from being God's access to my family.

We want to cooperate with God as he forms each person in our families to be a unique expression of himself, placed purposefully in his world.

We're concerned not only with the interests and drives of our family members but also with the kind of people they are becoming. We cooperate with God when we're up to the same thing he is and model what we know he's up to.

Want more patience in your family? To spread patience, you be more patient. Want people to care more about each other and put others first? Show what that looks like by modeling it rather than describing it.

Want less yelling? Want people to feel loved and appreciated? You don't need to give a speech, just start loving and appreciating, and watch love multiply over time.

These are just some of the character traits God desires in each of us. We know this because we see them in the Bible.

When we read the Bible, we see the big picture of what God is doing in each of us. And when we pay attention, we see what God is doing in each person's life through their unique drives and interests.

We put our families in a big bear hug when we unite the big-picture Bible things and the unique what-we-see-in-each-person things. We want to cooperate with God as he forms each person in our families to be a unique expression of himself, placed purposefully in his world.

What does it look like to cooperate with God?

Set the Pace with Your Own Walking

Remember the story of the guy with earbuds in the waiting room tapping his foot, and another guy tapping his foot along with him even though he couldn't hear the music? It takes only one person to hear the music. One person can set the pace, and others will keep pace with him even when they don't hear the music themselves.

What is the music that your family could walk along to with you? The Bible says, "Walk in a manner worthy of the calling to which you have been called" (Eph. 4:1). In other words, "Live like this. Be this type of person. This kind of person walks like this, keeps the rhythm."

God is speaking to all of us, so we know that includes the family, which just happens to be the most contagious social organization there is. Family members are wired to walk along with each other.

What does this walk look like? He tells us exactly in Ephesians 4: Be humble, patient, bearing with one another in love. Don't be consumed by anger. Let your words build up and give grace. Avoid bitterness, wrath, and malice. Be kind, tenderhearted, and forgiving. "Be this kind of person," God says. If everyone loved their family this way, the world would be different. If just one person in a family did this, that person could be a world changer.

Are you willing to cooperate with God and be a start-with-my-family world changer, no matter what anyone else does?

When you walk in a manner worthy of your calling, then you are God's access to your family. They hear his music through you. Since family is designed as the most contagious social unit there is, you will influence them.

You have no choice but to be an influence. The only choice you have is what kind of influence you will be. Part of your calling is to be God's access to your family. But that potential is fulfilled only when you walk in a manner worthy of that calling. Otherwise you're the access of something else, not of God. Dale Carnegie said, "Any fool can criticize, condemn, and complain. And most fools do."[2] Ouch. Who would want to walk along with that? We're wired to walk along with something; let's choose to walk God's way. How can we help our families want to walk along?

Be the Encourager

People in the human sciences work hard to understand and explain what God did when he made the world and wired us with certain defaults. The need for encouragement is one of those defaults. From what I've read, I've come to conclude that we need at least six times more encouragement than criticism. Scientific studies are always catching up with how God made us, and he made us to thrive under encouragement.

God's enemy is the accuser, the criticizer, the blamer, the discourager. God's enemy is the anti-encourager. I don't want to be my family's access to discouragement.

There is a place for blunt criticism and correction. Sometimes someone needs to hear, "You're heading for the ditch!" or "You just blew it" or "Stop before you make things worse." But these types of comments should be no more than one-sixth as much as the direct, blunt *encouragement* we receive. Encouragement should always outweigh criticism.

There are three problems with this.

One, criticism comes easily and naturally, so we underestimate how critical we actually are. We criticize more than we realize.

Two, criticism is often true! We're telling the truth when we criticize. Isn't the truth good? But it's not the whole truth, and there's often more to the story that sometimes explains or mitigates the criticism.

Three, we all automatically give more weight to criticism than to encouragement. That's why it takes five encouragements to equal one criticism, and six to outweigh the criticism so we *feel* encouraged. Someone can compliment you several times, but throw in one criticism and what's the thing you keep thinking about later? What's the thing you share with a friend? What's the thing that most influences how you feel? Criticism instantly gets our attention and keeps it.

We all naturally see faults. But majoring on finding faults is not God's way, and it doesn't produce what God desires. It doesn't change the person being criticized. If criticism produced change, you'd never have to say, "I've told you a million times! Will you ever learn?"

Majoring on criticism does accomplish one big thing: it steals energy from people. On the other hand, encouragement infuses energy into people.

You've seen this played out in your own childhood or in your own backyard. Two kids are running at the same speed, neck and neck. To one you yell, "I can't believe how slow you're going! You need to go faster! Is that all you can do? I thought you could do better than that!" And it's true, you do think they could do so much better.

> Other people's judgment exercises a paralyzing effect. Fear of criticism kills spontaneity; it prevents men from showing themselves and expressing themselves freely, as they are.
>
> Paul Tournier[3]

To the other kid you yell, "Way to go! Look at you! Awesome! You're running like the wind! Go, go, go, go!" This is true too.

If you were one of those kids, which phrases would energize you and make you try harder? All other things being equal, which kid do you think will win? Which kid will feel better?

Which kid will you have a better relationship with?

Would you rather *give* energy to those you love or *steal* it from them?

You don't improve relationships by pointing out faults and telling people how they need to change and how negatively they're affecting your life. They may need to change, they may have many faults, they may be negatively affecting your life, but repeatedly telling them won't fix things. Criticism is not a change agent. It's a venting agent for the criticizer.

Humans are wired to respond to love, grace, and respect. We are designed to become who we were created to be: beings in relationship with God who are being changed into his image and who walk in his ways. What are those ways again?

> *Criticism is not a change agent. It's a venting agent for the criticizer.*

Oh yeah: humility, patience, bearing with one another in love. Don't be consumed by anger. Let your words build up and give grace. Avoid bitterness, wrath, and malice. Be kind, tenderhearted, and forgiving. These are change agents. You are your family's access to these things and to God, and that access doesn't come through scolding and a wagging finger. Access comes through modeling the behavior you want to see.

Why are we so afraid of encouragement? Are we afraid the person receiving the encouragement will get a big head and stop trying?

One day I walked into the cleanest restroom I've ever seen in a fast-food place. I even looked for a urinal to make sure I hadn't accidentally walked into the ladies' room. Plants were perched on a table in the corner, and the whole place smelled like forsythia. Brenda said the women's restroom was the same. After we finished our Cajun biscuit and seasoned fries, Brenda found the cleaning lady and told her what a great job she was doing. The lady glowed and said she works only one day a week and tries to make that day special. Brenda made sure she knew it was.

After the compliments and encouragement, do you think she started slacking off?

Encouragement wins. When someone is specific and positive about who you are or how you do something, doesn't it make you want to be or do that even more? Encouragement energizes and inspires.

What do you spend more time doing in your family or in your most challenging relationships—correcting and pointing out short-comings or encouraging?

Be the Persuader toward What God Wants

"The Family Persuader" hung on the wall in our kitchen when I was growing up. It was a wooden paddle for dads, engraved with a silly poem that ended with advice to "hide this persuader" when Dad is the one messing up. Ha-ha. Dad never used it. He just liked the idea of it and thought the little rhyme was funny. Of course, there are other ways of looking at persuasion: "With patience a ruler may be persuaded, and a soft tongue will break a bone" (Prov. 25:15).

It's easy to like the idea of something. We all naturally like the idea of persuading. Don't you want people, especially family, to see things the same way you do? You know it would be good for them; if it wasn't good, you'd change your perspective, right? But persuading peoples' viewpoints doesn't change them on the inside; it doesn't touch their hearts and souls.

When Myquillyn and Emily were in their early teens, I liked the idea of a family Bible study. That's something a Christian family should do, right? So I bought the Scofield Study Bible for them and explained how it worked and how it was helpful. We had a little class on it. Then we had little classes on the Bible. That meant I talked, asked some questions, and they got bored. Hmmm.

I did it the way I thought was the only way—you sit down with a Bible and start talking. You don't consider them, or their day, or how they are feeling right now. You just teach the truth abstractly as you come across it. Teaching the Bible is essential, and that's one of the ways to do it.

While I believe the truth will apply itself to each person even if it's taught by *Ferris Bueller*'s Ben Stein, I also know that my way wasn't working with my kids. They were bored. It felt like they were just going through the motions. They couldn't relate. It wasn't the Bible's fault; it was mine. The Bible didn't talk to them; I did. But I didn't connect with them.

> People don't buy WHAT you do; they buy WHY you do it.
>
> Simon Sinek[4]

I thought since I was using the Bible, that was enough. That's what everyone says, right? *God's Word will not return void.* And I'm sure it didn't return void, but having a connecting experience with my family certainly did return void. I was a "Bible machine" spewing truth.

I think my mistake was that I swapped out being a dad—God's personal access to my family—for being a truth teller. What my family needed was someone they respected, someone who loved them, to share the truth in a personal way. What if, instead, I had said something like this:

> I lost my job today. I was freaked out for a while but then I remembered the Bible says that all things work for good to those who love God. And I remembered the Bible says that the king's heart is in the hand of the Lord and he turns it like a watercourse wherever he pleases. And I remember I'm to serve my employer as if I'm serving the Lord because the Lord is who I'm really working for. I've served as best I can, but now it looks like the Lord has turned my employer's heart.
>
> When I remember those things, I know I can feel just as confident unemployed as I felt employed because the Lord is in control and loves me. He's in the middle of this and knows what he's doing. The Lord is changing the assignment he has for me, and although I hate losing the job, I'm excited.

If we had had a family Bible time with that kind of conversation, I bet it would have felt very different to them. It would have felt personal, and they would have likely remembered it for a long time.

Of course, to say all that, I would have to believe it; I would have to personally engage the Bible and actually feel that way. It wouldn't do to say, "So here's how we as Christians should react in times of trials and tribulation."

To be God's access to your family, to be up to what he's up to, you need to allow him to have access to you first. You want to be up to what he's up to in your *own* life. You need to be a real, live, transparent person who deals with reality by faith and then shares that.

People are much more interested in our real lives than in our philosophy of life.

Be the Leader in the Messy Journey

One big thing we all have in common is this: we all know what it's like to be in the boat of messy reality, and we all long to see the shore from that boat.

Leadership goes far beyond family Bible time and is a key to any kind of persuasion we hope to accomplish in our families. It's about how we live with each other, love each other, and go through ordinary days together.

In a family, it's a lot more fun, and a lot more effective, to stop thinking of things we *should* do and instead think and live with the freedom and the honesty of messy reality. Being who you are is easier—and more persuasive—than being who you think you should be.

Leading the messy journey is a problem if you have trouble living with messy honesty. It's hard to welcome the mess if you insist on seeing yourself as some perfect stereotype of a successful mom, dad, or family member. If you insist on seeing yourself as you *should* be, then that's how you talk about things, and that's what you tell others. Your expectations of what should be leads to disconnection in relationships.

One of the most powerful things in the world is telling stories that reveal the reality of your mess *even while maintaining hope.* You admit that you can't control things, but you share how you find encouragement anyway. People hear that. This is much more persuasive than just a general admission of "Well, you know I'm not perfect."

Being who you are is easier—and more persuasive—than being who you think you should be.

This means you have to learn how to deal with messy reality and still somehow find encouragement—challenging but doable.

As I write this, I'm dealing with the loss of a job—again. I told myself that if I'm going to talk to people about hope, then I need to be an example of it. No moping around, no bitterness, and no faking it allowed. You can't say anything to anyone else that you haven't been challenged to live yourself. This responsibility inspires and challenges me. But it's no different from all the other everyday challenges that families face.

The most powerful hope you can share is the hope you have found yourself. People can tell when it's just talk. Of course, we can share hope we haven't yet found ourselves—but we should do it gently and humbly, acknowledging our need for that same hope as cotravelers. No raised finger "as Christians we need to . . ." attitudes allowed.

> He is able to deal gently with those who are ignorant and are going astray, since he himself is subject to weakness. (Heb. 5:2 NIV)

> That is why, for Christ's sake, I delight in weaknesses, in insults, in hardships, in persecutions, in difficulties. For when I am weak, then I am strong. (2 Cor. 12:10 NIV)

Imagine someone in your family—your spouse, parent, mother-in-law, sister, or even your nemesis—majoring in encouragement and giving it at least six times more than they criticize. How would that feel? How would it give you hope in your messiness?

Imagine getting the sense that this person sincerely cares about you, notices your interests and feelings, and truly wants what's best for you. Imagine that person humbly and transparently sharing the ups and downs of their own life and faith.

What difference would this make to you? What difference could it make in your family? That's the difference *you* can make when you cooperate with God and are his access to your family.

Your own life is a powerful picture that God can use as a model of what he wants to see. Powerful doesn't mean perfect, just perfectly usable. Since your family is created to be contagious, family members are already "catching" your life. Why not choose some things on purpose for them to catch? In the next chapter, you'll see how modeling includes telling, but in a more fun and natural way, and relieves you of the frustration of saying the same thing repeatedly.

— 11 —

Model What You Want to See

Show What It Looks Like

Home is life's undress rehearsal, its backroom, its dressing room.

Harriet Beecher Stowe

My parents told me with a shrug. Remember when I was sixteen and wanted to help them with their budget, and I told them they didn't have enough money? They shrugged—yeah, we know—and I believed I had discovered a truth of adulthood: you can't change the way things are. Believing that shrug may seem foolish, but you never know how or when an event or chance remark can take root in someone. I believed it up until I began discovering the *Timeless Tools*.

My best friend's mom told him with words. She made some negative predictions about him when he was a kid—the usual kinds of careless, throwaway, you'll-never-amount-to-anything stuff. Decades later, none of those predictions came true. But my friend still believes them—it *feels* like they're true.

I have another friend who recently found a page from a scratch pad on the kitchen table titled "Words that describe me." It was her daughter's note. She had written the words *awesome, responsible, silly,* and *persevering* on the paper. My friend got

> *The real telling is in the living, and no one sees the living like family. You can't fool family.*

weepy when she read it. "I realized these are words she heard from me."

We tell with words, we tell with attitudes, we tell with reactions, we tell with our behavior, we tell with our demeanor. Our lives are big telling machines.

Most of us act as if the only time we're telling is when we use words to instruct or correct or criticize or philosophize. It's enticing to be the expert or the authority and to pontificate on what to do and how. It makes me chuckle when I'm around someone I know well who's pontificating as an expert on a topic but who doesn't do what they preach. Oops, maybe that's just me.

The real telling is in the living, and no one sees the living like family. You can't fool family.

Back in my radio days, one of our on-air personalities read David Platt's *Radical* and said, "We need to tell everyone this message!" I suggested letting the message affect his life and then sharing his changed life on the radio. Isn't that how Platt wrote the book? Would you like a radio DJ telling you how to live?

Would you like a family member telling you how to live? We do it all too often. It's our default method of influence. What if there was a better way?

Woo More, Scold Less

Telling others what to do and telling them when they're wrong is the easy, everybody-does-it way that never seems to really work. I can scold and criticize like a pro without even trying. Sometimes without realizing it, I even do it when someone's trying to help me, taking over what they're doing, as if I know best. Correcting, criticizing, and scolding sometimes have their place, but they should never be our default mode.

Wooing hearts is the tougher, riskier way and takes longer, but it brings true satisfaction. Wooing feels like an invitation to join. Others are free to reject the invitation, but because they have a choice, they're actually more likely to accept. Wooing slips in the back door saying something *could* be; scolding barges in the front door saying something *should* be. The power of wooing is in its non-agenda. When I woo, you feel like I have nothing personally at stake in your response. It gives you permission to focus on what's in your own best interest.

> *Wooing slips in the back door saying something* could *be; scolding barges in the front door saying something* should *be.*

Modeling is wooing. It works far better for influencing behavior and attitudes than lecturing or scolding. When the kids get older and look over your shoulder from the back seat and see that you're speeding, do you think when they get behind the wheel that they'll be influenced more by what they saw or what you say? Modeling takes humility and hard work. Jesus modeled this in his life, and because he's made our families to be contagious, they will catch this too.

Modeling instead of pushing, pointing, repeating, and correcting is how we can be up to what God is up to—and is how we fulfill our role as God's access to our families. We already know what he's up to because it's the same thing we want: more patience, more feeling loved and appreciated, more caring about one another and putting others first, less yelling. We know what to do.

Modeling Appreciation

When Mr. Rogers won the Lifetime Achievement Emmy Award in 1997, his gentle acceptance speech transformed a glitzy, self-focused industry celebration into a calm gathering of generosity and appreciation.

> So many people have helped me to come to this night.
> Some of you are here. Some are far away. Some are even in heaven.
> All of us have special ones who have loved us into being.
> Would you just take, along with me, ten seconds to think of the people who have helped you become who you are?
> Those who have cared about you and wanted what was best for you in life.
> Ten seconds of silence. I'll watch the time . . . (He looks down at his watch for ten seconds.)
> Whomever you've been thinking about, how pleased they must be to know the difference you feel they've made.[1]

At first you hear a slight awkward shock that he's making his moment about everyone else. Then the camera pans to show tears, introspective looks, emotional smiles. His gentle demeanor and sincere appreciation become contagious. For a minute, the room is filled with the humanity of gratitude. All from one man. Imagine the same transformation in your family.

Mr. Rogers was always the same, whether talking to our kids through the TV or talking to Hollywood stars. It takes a lot of your family's energy to figure out which you is the real you.

Mr. Rogers didn't talk about being calm; he *was* calm. He didn't talk about the need to be calm; he lived it. Talking goes to the head; "being" goes to the heart and inspires.

He also modeled giving credit to others even though he was the one who deserved it, *especially* when he deserved it. We know instinctively that it feels better to give credit than to take it. He created an opportunity for others to give credit, and we can do the same. We can create opportunities and expectations for our families to purposefully express gratitude for the help of others. Your family will imitate you. You'll hardly ever need to push or lecture.

This is how we love someone into being and help them become who they are.

Modeling Humility

It's probably not tough to say to a family member:

"Isn't this fun!"

"Please pass the beets."

"Yes, I took out the garbage."

When something is fun, lighthearted, informational, or gives you the credit, it's easy to say it.

Unfortunately, it's also probably not hard to say:

"I can't believe you said that!"

"You *never* give me credit for anything!"

"I hate you!"

Those things can come out all too easily, no thinking or effort required. They burst out driven by our emotions. We have to work *not* to say them. But you might find it difficult to say:

"You are *so* good at that!"

"I need you."

"You make my life better."

Why is it easier to say something hurtful than to say something that builds someone up? This is where we get a clue to that nasty default built into us: judging others and demanding justice of others. We're born selfish and judgmental. No child needs to be taught to say, "Mine!" or "No fair!"

> *Being right is fun. Being humble is godly.*

Your hardest thing to say may be different from mine. But whatever it is, I'll bet it requires humility. Here's the toughest thing for me to say to a family member: "You were right. I was wrong."

More and more with my wife, Brenda, I seem to be wrong. I'm getting really good at it. Shouldn't I be getting better at being right? Maybe I am, but perhaps she's getting there faster than I am.

Being wrong gets your attention. The more convinced you are that you are right, the more being wrong gets your attention, and the harder it is to backtrack. Backtracking is not fun. The more you backtrack, the more sensitive you are to overconfidence. Sensitivity to overconfidence is good.

"I'm sorry" is much easier for me to say than "You were right. I was wrong." Both parts together are the kicker. You humble yourself while raising the other up. This goes against everything built into you at birth. But it goes *with* everything put into you through faith in Jesus.

> In humility count others more significant than yourselves. (Phil. 2:3)

> God opposes the proud but gives grace to the humble. (James 4:6)

> Everyone who exalts himself will be humbled, but the one who humbles himself will be exalted. (Luke 18:14)

Being right is fun. Being humble is godly. We're always modeling one or the other.

Modeling Perspective

If anyone deserved to be yelled at, corrected, criticized, and scolded, it was Ebenezer Scrooge. You could have said to him till you were blue in the face, "You need to be kinder and gentler. People matter! It's not all about work! How can you treat Bob Cratchit like that—he's hurting. His son's sick. You're wasting your life!" All that was true. But telling someone they should change hardly ever changes anything.

What Ebenezer does comes from somewhere—his inner scrooge, a view, a perspective, an expectation of life. What he does makes perfect sense to him—it fits his perspective, his expectation. In a way, he can't do anything different; it's outside his realm of experience and comprehension.

> *Telling someone they should change hardly ever changes anything.*

Then one night he's confronted with a new perspective. He meets three guides who show him his life from a view outside himself. He's never seen his own life from this angle. It's so radically different that he's traumatized, and he begs for them to stop. His eyes are opened, and what he does, how he acts, and the kind of person he is changes.

If you want to influence a spouse, parent, mother- or daughter-in-law, grown child, or any family member, one way is to help them see things from a different point of view. Don't make change the issue. Instead, guide like the three ghosts of Christmas.

Perspective is "the ability to perceive things in their actual interrelationships of comparative importance."[2] I've also heard it said that perspective is when little things are seen for what they really are. We need guides to help us see.

My friend Harold rarely gave me the answer or told me to change. But he was wonderful at guiding me into adjusting my camera angle. He helped me see by modeling how he saw things and allowed time for my perspective to change.

Modeling Wooing

I knew some pushy Christians back when I was an outsider. A few were so relentless that I once said the prayer of salvation just to get them off my back. "Just say this prayer," they kept saying. But a minute later, I took the prayer back. They went away confused. A few years later, alone, I said the prayer for the right reasons, responding to God's wooing.

Being pushy is not the same thing as being direct or persuasive. Pushy can make you react to the one pushing rather than responding to the thing being pushed. Sometimes you don't even notice the thing they're pushing because you're so bugged by how they're doing it.

I thought about that when I read how Keith Richards of the Rolling Stones fell in love with the guitar. His grandpa Gus *wanted* Keith to fall in love with the guitar, but he didn't push it. He did the opposite. Every time little kid Keith would visit, Gus would put a guitar on top of the piano.

> The guitar was totally out of reach. It was something you looked at, thought about, but never got your hands on.
>
> I'll never forget the guitar on top of his upright piano every time I'd go and visit, starting maybe from the age of five. I thought that was where the thing lived. I thought it was always there. And I just kept looking at it, and he didn't say anything, and a few years later I was still looking at it. "Hey, when you get tall enough, you can have a go at it," he said.
>
> I didn't find out until after he was dead that he only brought that out and put it up there when he knew I was coming to visit. So I was being teased in a way.[3]

One day Gus finally did take the guitar down and give it to Keith. He's never been without a guitar since.

Gus knew what he wanted. He also knew his grandson. He knew the guitar had to be Keith's idea, and Keith would have to be hungry for it. Wooing is risky because the other person may not respond in the way we desire. But there's no guarantee with pushing either. I took banjo lessons when I was a kid because my dad pushed me into it. I don't play the banjo today. You probably share some similar stories.

A rich guy came to Jesus thinking he wanted Jesus. The guy went away sad when he realized he couldn't want money and Jesus equally. Jesus didn't chase him. He knew it wouldn't do any good. You don't grab a life preserver unless you know you're drowning, and the rich guy didn't yet know he was drowning. Jesus stayed where he was, like the guitar on the piano.

When you model wooing, you create an accepting, trusting atmosphere that honors the one you are wooing. Then the wooing itself becomes contagious and can become a way of life in your family.

Modeling the Value of Bonding

My wife, Brenda, is selling a desk for $125. A buyer is coming to see it, so before he gets here, I role-play with her. "I'll give you $75."

"One-ten," she says. We go back and forth like that a little longer just for practice.

The buyer gets here and likes the desk. "Would you take . . ."—all right, here comes the beat down—"One-fifteen?"

"Uh, sure!" Almost full price. Great.

He unfolds the cash and starts talking about how he'll get the desk in his little car.

Brenda pipes up, "You know what? I'll take a hundred. OK?" She's lowering the price. She's bargaining with herself, to her own disadvantage.

The buyer's confused. He stammers like Brenda did, "Uh, sure!"

Later, she says she could tell he wanted to say one hundred when he first came in, but he just couldn't. Because he offered more and was willing to lose on the price, she felt free to give him what he didn't ask for.

When you start to open a door and there's resistance, what do you do? Push harder. And when you're on the other side and a door is opening into you, it's the same—you naturally push back. When the pusher lets up, so do you.

That holds true for more than just money and doors. Think of anything in your family where some kind of persuading is going on—for example, a disagreement on a new house or planning a vacation or where to eat tonight.

You can turn things into a negotiation to get the best deal, and you'll get some kind of deal. Or you can make things about relationship and get some kind of connection and affirmation.

Want the best deal? Want to get your way? Try to win. Make the deal the goal.

Want connection and bonding? Be willing to lose. Make bonding the goal.

You get to choose.

When you put people first, when you become known for doing that, what do you think will happen in your family when there's a negotiation of some kind? They will start to value bonding over winning, just like you modeled.

Modeling the Value of a Person

My friend bought tickets to see Billy Joel and Elton John in Charlotte. He had connections and was able to get seventh-row seats. Yes, they cost him. But he's a Billy Joel fan and was excited about being "close enough to count his nose hairs!"

He got the tickets two months in advance. A week out he realized his seven-year-old daughter had a recital the same night.

What did he do?

That's a no-brainer. He went to the recital. He didn't even have to think about it. He never thought about it while at the recital, either. He sold the tickets and so wasn't out the money, but he was out the experience.

He hasn't told his daughter. He's afraid she'll feel bad that he missed the concert. One day he will tell her, and he'll have a choice of two good messages to send.

He could say, "I didn't go because I sacrificed for you"—and her response will be, "You'd do that for me?" It will be a great message to her about how much he loves her.

Or he could say, "I didn't go because I wanted to see you more"— and her response will be, "I'm that valuable?" With this message, not going to the concert wasn't even a sacrifice because he didn't lose by not going; he got something better—her.

My friend told me why he didn't have to even think about it. *His dad did the same thing*—"He never put himself before us." His dad didn't teach it, lecture it, or tell it. He just did it. And my friend caught what his dad was infected with. I'll bet his kids will be infected too.

Modeling Can Seem Slow and Fruitless

Modeling doesn't give the immediate buzz of satisfaction that comes with telling, criticizing, or scolding. That satisfaction is short-lived, however, because you soon discover that you need to keep telling, criticizing, or scolding, since they rarely change anything. Because modeling takes effect at a slower pace, it may seem pointless at first, until you get the first hint of change—someone uses a phrase you used, or the usual blow-up doesn't materialize. Modeling requires faith, patience, and perseverance, all of which God desires in us. Do you think maybe he's using modeling as much for your good as for your family's?

One thing to consider during the slow process of modeling is something Oswald Chambers says: "God rarely allows a soul to see how great a blessing he is."[4] If that's true, then whatever blessing you think your influence has been is not the blessing you have really been. You think you're a blessing through your official duties as a parent or spouse or family member—the thing that's your role and that you work for.

What if, instead, the blessing you are is your presence and the invisible uniqueness of Jesus in you personally? Sure, what you do counts, and it can count immensely. But there's more to it than that. We go back to some words from Chambers that you read at the end of chapter 2:

> A river touches places of which its source knows nothing, and Jesus says if we have received of His fullness, however small the visible measure of our lives, out of us will flow the rivers that will bless to the uttermost parts of the earth.

The river of the fullness of Jesus in you is touching your family through your simple presence. Stay in the river. Show up and be yourself. This is your ministry.

— 12 —

Release Your Family, Your Role, and the Results into God's Hands

He Wants More for Your Family Than You Do

> He who did not spare his own Son but gave him up for us all, how will he not also with him graciously give us all things?
>
> Romans 8:32

We're finishing our journey down the momentum-gathering river. We began with trusting God for getting our peace right. Now we come full circle with trusting God by releasing everything into his hands.

The Family Relationships Expert

Back when James Dobson had his radio show *Focus on the Family*, I heard that people would call the ministry after the program to talk to Dr. Dobson about their parenting questions. Of course, given his leadership level at the ministry, he couldn't take time to answer phone calls. So they compiled all the advice and answers from his books into a database so that anyone answering calls had access to what Dr. Dobson would say. Still, callers wanted to talk to him personally—they needed reassurance that they were getting his exact advice for their specific problems.

Every one of us wants this. If only we had access to someone who is not only experienced but also knows us and each member of our families and all the details of what's happened and how we got here. Someone who could tell us what to do in the midst of our problems. Mom? Mom would be great—but maybe she's tangled up in everything too. Or gone. Or part of the problem.

Over the years we've done our best, but it falls short. We've got the experience, the desire, the ability. Some say we're way above average in these areas, but it's still not enough.

> [Jesus] sat down and taught the people from the boat. And when he had finished speaking, he said to Simon, "Put out into the deep and let down your nets for a catch."
>
> And Simon answered, "Master, we toiled all night and took nothing! But at your word I will let down the nets."
>
> And when they had done this, they enclosed a large number of fish, and their nets were breaking. They signaled to their partners in the other boat to come and help them. And they came and filled both the boats, so that they began to sink. (Luke 5:3–7)

Jesus was not a dad, never toilet trained a kid or waited up for a daughter. He never lost his temper and had to live with regret. He never fixed a flat tire or planned a budget or felt rejected by a mother-in-law. Nor was he an expert fisherman. But he told the experts where to catch fish, and they did. More than they could catch on their own.

Sometimes when I'm doing a project at home and lose a screw or can't make something fit together, I ask Jesus to help me. Isn't that trivial? Asking the almighty God of the universe for help with a little screw? Something good always happens, though. I do that less often when I'm lost on the road because, you know, I'm a guy. It seems I do it even less with the big stuff.

He's not an expert or master because of experience but because he is deity. He is one of a kind.

Need Results?

For years you've tried; you've put in the work. You've followed the guidance you could find. And little has changed. Is it a waste? Do you quit? What do you do when your work seems fruitless? It's hard to hope when there's nothing to show for your efforts.

> The Son can do nothing by himself; he can only do what he sees his Father doing. (John 5:19 NIV)

> I am the vine; you are the branches. Whoever abides in me and I in him, he it is that bears much fruit, for apart from me you can do nothing. (John 15:5)

Of course, Jesus did things differently than I do. He is deity, yet he didn't go off on his own but only did what he saw "his Father doing." I am not God, but I often trust in myself as if I were!

This isn't advice, but it makes sense to me: when I feel fruitless, I've said to God out loud, "You say that if I abide in you, that if I stay in you and find my source of living in you, I *will* bear fruit. So, Lord, either I'm bearing fruit and you just don't want me to see it, or I'm *not* remaining and abiding in you." I have to keep it simple.

To remain in him, I continue to keep it simple. I trust him and his love and his purpose. I follow the best I can. I don't try to earn results by performing or doing some ritual like keeping a quiet time; I keep my quiet time to help me remain in him. Remaining is trusting.

I try to trust simply for the next step and then take it. And to continue to trust no matter what is seen or not seen. I try to trust not for particular results but only for my personal relationship with him. Everything else I release to him. Our relationship is the biggest result.

Four Things to Release, and What Releasing Could Look Like

1. Release your family (and your nemesis).

Lord, you created them and made us each to be a gift to each other. Thank you. They were not my idea, and I was not my idea. I did not bring my family together, and I cannot keep them together. You can do anything you want with each of them and with me. Help me see everything that's good in each one and in our family as a whole.

Thank you that you don't want me burdened with the responsibility for how everything turns out, and thank you that you're always creating circumstances and allowing troubles that pressure me to release them to you. Forgive me for trying to own them and our relationships. You take them; they're yours. And please remind me tomorrow to release them to you again. And I give _____ to you for you to do anything you want, even if you want to leave everything the same.

2. Release your role.

Thank you, Lord, for creating a clear dividing line between what you do and what I do. You are in charge of results; I'm in charge of my effort within my role—thank you that

167

I at least know that much. Thank you for making my role so easy when I cooperate with you and when I model and act as an example rather than scold, criticize, and correct. Thank you that crossing over to your role produces stress and frustration. Help me know that the answer is not to try or push harder but to stay in my role and woo. And thank you that the boundary lines have fallen for me in pleasant places.

3. Release your limits.

It's funny how I can be so self-critical and beat myself up over my shortcomings yet act as if I know it all when it comes to how others should act and who they should be. OK, it's not funny. I get frustrated from

> *Thank you that my limits are the beginning of your life being revealed in my mortal body.*

trying and failing, but then, Lord, you remind me that you didn't create me to be successful at fixing people or relationships. Why don't you remind me of that before I try so hard? Oh yeah, you do but I don't listen. Thank you that you have made my weakness perfect in your strength. Thank you that my limits are the beginning of your life being revealed in my mortal body.

4. Release the results.

One more time, Lord: you're in charge of results; I'm in charge of my effort within my role. Thank you that you always know what's best and want what's best and that you can bring it about even when I butt in. Sometimes, Lord, I act as if releasing control is a sacrifice that I have to do as an act of faith out of obedience. In reality, releasing is a relief. It's a gift. And when I refuse to release control, what am I saying? That you can't handle it? That you're not trustworthy? Surely I'm not saying that. Thank you that you've graciously set things up so that when I try to take charge of results, you back off so that I can see the difference between your results and mine. Thank you that it's such a big difference.

Instead of Control

Prayer is the most practical thing you can do for your family. Prayer is not abstract theory or an idea or philosophy or strategy. It's not what you do when nothing else works. You think of prayer as a spiritual thing, and it is, but it's a spiritual thing in action with practical results.

When our girls were little, Brenda began praying for their husbands. Years later, it was freaky at the wedding rehearsal dinner

In reality, releasing is a relief. It's a gift.

seeing the tables with the pictures of Myquillyn and Chad growing up separately and thinking, *So that's what he looked like and was doing when she was this age* . . . and realizing that Brenda was praying for him all that time without knowing who he was.

A few years ago Brenda and I wanted to pray more consistently. So we made it as easy and automatic as we could: we don't get up from eating together at home without praying. So at the end of almost every meal at home, before we clean up, we push the plates away, hold hands, and pray for two or five or ten minutes. We keep it short, simple, and consistent. Our peace and confidence have greatly increased.

Our peace and confidence don't come from getting results. Most of the time I'm surprised when I see my prayers answered positively. Many

Prayer is reaching out for God and the unseen.

Andrew Murray[1]

are not, and that seems normal; even God's negative answers are as good as the positive ones because he always has my best interest in mind.

Our peace comes from the practical act of cooperating with God in reaching out for the unseen good we want for our family—and knowing he will do something. And our peace comes from personal intimacy with the almighty God of the universe, who rules over heaven and earth yet knows the number of hairs on my head and when a sparrow falls to the ground.

Recently, we prayed every day for three months to know what to do in an area I was restless about. It was a big deal to me. I wrote bullet points on what we were praying for, and why, and printed a copy for each of us. I never got a direct answer, but the restlessness ceased, and I've moved on with peace and confidence.

> *Our peace comes from personal intimacy with the almighty God of the universe, who rules over heaven and earth yet knows the number of hairs on my head.*

Then there was that day when I wanted some family members to talk about something important to all of us. But I was busy and stressed and had no time or words to start a conversation. In frustration, I said a brief prayer alone and gave it to God and headed to work. By the time I got home, they had talked.

One more thing—beware of PWD. Your prayer life can be defeated by it: Prayer Warrior Disease. PWD convinces you that no matter how often or how long you pray, it's never enough. You are just a loser, and you're discouraged from praying. Seriously, this is as common as a cold.

If you suffer from PWD, here's the cure: when you're watching TV or a movie, during a commercial or a break, turn the sound down and pray for one minute. Too long? Try thirty seconds. If you're married, hold hands and pray out loud and thank God for your spouse. That's *all*. Stop.

Then tomorrow do the same thing, and pray about something else for your family for one minute. This is the cure for PWD. Once it's cured, you can move on with your prayer life in the times and places that are natural for you and your family.

Release Control

In my radio days, whenever I did an interview with someone who was sharing advice, I would ask them one bottom-line question as a simple takeaway for people.

One time I asked John Fuller from Focus on the Family, "What is one thing that would make the biggest or quickest difference in parenting—one attitude or thing parents could do?"

He didn't pause a second: "Give up control."

He said our kids have a thing called free will that will destroy all our expectations of control. Amen to that, right? And every family member has that free will too.

How can we have reasonable expectations for discerning the control we have and don't have? For me, I picture the dentist's chair. That chair reminds me that we're a partnership but with a sharp division of roles. If we get our role mixed up with the dentist's role, we'll be confused, frustrated, and fruitless. And our teeth will hurt.

You know the roles: You have to show up—but someone else does the real work. You put yourself in someone else's hands—but you're still deeply involved. You're not the one in control—but you can resist and fight and hinder the one who is.

In the dentist's office, you know you're not the expert. You would never say, "Give me that drill, I'll do it." But neither are you passive. You don't just flop and expect things to happen. You keep the appointment. You rearrange things to be there. You do what they say. You open wide. You spit. You are aware of everything that's going on. Then you go home and you brush and floss as you've been instructed.

Yes, you're definitely fully involved. There's a cost to you. But you're not the one doing the work—someone else accomplishes it.

What are you trying to make happen that only God can make happen? As author and speaker Beth Moore has said,

> I am not in control.
> I cannot control all my people.
> I cannot control our situation . . . even when I want what's best.
> I cannot control the outcome.

I cannot make people behave.

I cannot make people believe.

I cannot make people be strong . . . because I am not God.

He alone knows the end from the beginning.

He alone knows how this thing will turn out.

I hereby fire myself from his job.

I agree to see my fight for control as what it really is . . . a screaming testament to my distrust.[2]

As we've made our way together down the momentum-gathering river, we've looked closely at many of the *Timeless Tools of Family Peace*. We've seen how the *Timeless Tools* can work together, reinforce each other, and build momentum in our families.

We've realized the great power that comes from a peaceful attitude of trust and have found moments to give genuine attention to others, knowing it's an act of love as well as an act of curiosity about what God is up to in each family member's life. These are the first attitudes and acts of a person cooperating with God, no matter what family we're in. This is the beginning of modeling for our families. And these are things that can become contagious.

After a bit of peace and trust, attention and curiosity, you begin to notice more things God is up to in your family, and you get more ideas for little ways to cooperate. In part 3, I'll try to help you get even more specific about what the *Timeless Tools* can look like in your family situation.

Part 3

YOUR FAMILY RIVER

The only way to live a remarkable life is not to get everyone to notice you, but to leave noticeable marks of love everywhere you go. You love as well as you are willing to be inconvenienced.

It's never too late to live a remarkable life. Just start leaving marks of love now—right when it's inconvenient. And then tomorrow. Not twenty years from now. Not two weeks from now. Now. Right now. Always in the inconvenient right now.

Ann Voskamp

— 13 —

Drops of Grace into Your River

Find Ways to Be Your Family's Biggest Fan

The best and most beautiful things in the world cannot be seen nor touched, but are felt in the heart.

Helen Keller

Little, practical drops of grace over time create ripples that can become waves and eventually a tide. A drop of grace might be one of the *Timeless Tools*, or it might be a small touch that's consistent with the *Timeless Tools*.

Because I believe in Jesus, the starting point for grace is very elemental. It's Coke fountain syrup. It's OxiClean powder waiting for water. It's over-the-top radical: I don't get hell, even though I deserve it. I do get heaven, even though I don't deserve it. And all the spiritual people say, yes!

Then I go out and water it down or divorce it from my life. What would grace look like in my family if it was not diluted? Oswald Chambers once said, "Never look for justice in this world, but never cease to give it."[1] The expectation and hunger for justice from others is behind every frustration, harsh word, argument, and family estrangement. Each one of us thinks, *It's not fair, and it's more unfair to me than you.*

But grace says, "I won't give you the bad I think you deserve, and I will give you the good you don't." It's so radical and potent that just a few drops can begin to infect an entire family. To start, maybe I pause a few seconds to reflect before I defend myself—because you might be right. Later, I may be able to pause longer. Maybe I relax one little expectation I have of how you'll treat me.

Maybe during one disagreement I keep my mouth shut and let you totally have your say. I don't argue, even with my inner voice. In fact, I'm surprised by a feeling of strength and calm. Suddenly, in a way, it's OK if I don't convince you I'm right. It feels kind of good!

Grace wins by satisfying you with itself. Then grace wins by spreading.

That's when you begin to discover that grace wins. It doesn't win by winning the argument or meeting the expectation. Grace wins by satisfying you with itself. Then grace wins by spreading.

Grace can begin one small drop at a time. What might one drop of letting go of justice look like for you and your family?

Drops of Generosity

Remember Brenda's desk story? The guy offered $115. She said no, I'll take less. Get it? The seller talked the buyer *down.*

She did it because she had a good feeling about him; he was meek, not pushy. One drop of letting go of justice. One drop of grace. One drop of generosity.

I saw the same thing on *American Pickers* recently. The seller took Mike and Frank's first offer almost every time. Once in a while he negotiated a bit. Mike and Frank were pumped at the great stuff they were getting.

At the end of the show before they left, they gave the seller an extra $400, which was not what he was expecting. "You gave us some awesome deals," Mike said. "Take the money, we're still going to make a good profit." They had to argue with the seller to get him to take the cash.

What might one drop of letting go of justice look like for you and your family?

Generosity is built into you and your family. It causes people to want to reciprocate. Of course, the messiness of life—suspicion, fear, anger, busyness, bitterness, fatigue—often interferes. Reciprocation is not always an automatic response, and it may not occur right away.

But be confident that when you are generous, you are cooperating and trusting a great law of creation that is built into humans. God has made us automatically sensitive to generosity so that we're sensitized to his generosity to us in Christ.

Generosity is part of God's image, and he has stamped us with his image. The image is corrupted by the fall, and we're all now naturally selfish, but the seed and echo of generosity remain. Water the seed with drops of grace to get generosity growing.

To fight the voice in you that says, "Good idea; I'll do it later," start small. Find the teeniest, least noticeable way to be generous to your family, and try to do it so they won't initially even be aware. Bite your tongue. Smile when you don't feel like it. Subtly step aside. Take the smaller piece. Be gentle for a moment when you're normally hard.

You know your family—make a small but meaningful gesture to one of them. Keeping it small helps you get started.

My brother the landscaper told me about how he controls the growth of trees and shrubs on his property. He said that no matter how hard he works, plants will always do what they are wired to do, even growing through concrete sometimes. So he's learned not to fight the plants but to cooperate with their growth patterns, planting them in places that fit their wiring.

> Courtesies of a small and trivial character are the ones which strike deepest in the grateful and appreciating heart.
>
> Henry Clay[2]

When you do small, consistent acts of generosity for your family, you are cooperating with something that is already at work in them. Over time they may begin to reciprocate. Then, when you get a little more momentum going, some good things will come. The Bible tells us, "Whoever sows sparingly will also reap sparingly, and whoever sows bountifully will also reap bountifully" (2 Cor. 9:6).

What's the smallest, most invisible act of generosity you could do for a family member today?

Drops of Humor

My wife says we're closer than we've ever been. Why? "You laugh at my funny stuff now. You never used to laugh." I could argue and say, "Well, you weren't funny then; now you are," but that's just defensiveness.

Humor connects people. Everybody says they want a connected family more than anything, but when given the choice of taking offense or defusing a situation with humor, we almost always take offense. I sometimes think we must all have a secret love of being offended; we grab every opportunity to be "hurt":

I can't believe you said that.

You never care what I think.

What am I, chopped liver?!

I'm tired of putting up with this/being ignored/always being the one to . . .

It takes humility and courage not to take offense. Next time you are confronted with a possible offense, try one of the following:

- Don't fight or bristle or disagree. Go along with the comment or thing that irks you.
- Be lighthearted.
- Pretend this is a game in which you're confident and unhurtable.
- Jokingly mock and disarm the potential offense by exaggerating it, then turn it into something positive, without making any derogatory comment.
- Picture this instead: it's not an offense; it's a puffy, colorful beach ball! Let it bounce off you and playfully head back to them.

Following are a couple examples of someone giving you the opportunity to be offended and how humor can derail trouble:

Them: "That was so ridiculous I don't even know what you just said."

You: "Well, you should replay the tape because it was genius." And smile.

Them: "Wow—the candles on your birthday cake could heat the whole house!"

You: "I know! If you're lucky, you'll have that many one day and still look this good."

One time at breakfast my boss mentioned something that bothered him about a coworker, and two of us cautiously pointed out that he did the same thing. "I do? (scary pause) Well, I guess I just need to keep quiet and eat my biscuit . . ." Defused. No offense. Nothing personal.

My wife and I are much better at this today. In the old days, we took everything so seriously. Today, when one of us says something that could be taken offensively, the other will say quietly and mockingly serious, "You just need to SHUT. UP." It's an inside joke, reminding us of how much we've changed since the days when our attitudes toward each other were harsh and negative. We never say it in front of anyone else. Sometimes we'll add "and eat your biscuit" in honor of my boss. It's our secret code for *I'm giving you grace and I will not let this turn into anything.*

You don't have to be an expert at this, just successful enough to keep offenses from dominating.

Drops of Grace at Family Gatherings

A friend told me he wasn't attending an annual family get-together. "The rest of the family can't get along during the year, and I can't stand watching everyone try to be nice to each other. I'm sick of it." Can you relate?

I shared that story with Brenda at breakfast and asked rhetorically, "So what can you do when your family is difficult, argumentative, critical, negative, and everybody's always getting their feelings hurt—and then you all vacation or take a holiday together?"

She started talking and I grabbed a notecard to make notes. I had a few thoughts too. Maybe one of these will add some calm and encouragement to your next family gathering:

1. Take charge of making people feel wanted. Find little ways to show some excitement and appreciation for each person's presence. Start now, before they arrive. You want them to feel like their presence matters to you.

2. Don't expect your words to have the power to fix everything. You're not going to repair years of family dysfunction on one day. But positive, encouraging words *can* keep things from getting worse and can set a mood and tone for conversations.

3. Don't look at this gathering as a chance to talk about Christianity to your relatives. (Of course, if they bring it up, go for it.) Take it as a chance to *model* Christianity. Show up as your normal self and don't underestimate the power of Jesus in you.

4. Be a master of patience and calm. Don't let your mood or tone be influenced by any chaotic negativity. Don't try to fix things, don't scold, don't get huffy or flustered on the outside. Calm silence is powerful over the long haul.

5. After a meal, while still at the table, go around and share one thing you appreciate about the individual on your left. You start. Keep it short and sincere. Maybe try it again at another meal.

6. Think of this gathering as just one click on the family-togetherness dial. Then later, build on that small improvement in the dial position. More opportunities for clicks are coming at future gatherings.

7. Spend some time before you get together pondering the following words:

> Do not let any unwholesome talk come out of your mouths, but only what is helpful for building others up according to their needs, that it may benefit those who listen. (Eph. 4:29 NIV)

> Do all things without grumbling or disputing, that you may be blameless and innocent, children of God without blemish in the midst of a crooked and twisted generation, among whom you shine as lights in the world. (Phil. 2:14–15)

For where jealousy and selfish ambition exist, there will be disorder and every vile practice. But the wisdom from above is first pure, then peaceable, gentle, open to reason, full of mercy and good fruits, impartial and sincere. And a harvest of righteousness is sown in peace by those who make peace. (James 3:16–18)

Family get-togethers can be full of potential and yet be challenging. All the old hurts and agendas are waiting in the wings to pounce and take over. Faces are reminders of past hurts and injustices. And everyone pushed together creates opportunities for new offenses.

Can you resist the urge to dish out justice? Joseph believed Mary was pregnant by another man. Yet he would not publicly and shamefully send her away, even though it looked like she deserved it. Of course, it turned out things were not at all how they looked. The argument, the slight, the insult, the offense may beg for retaliation, but for these few days of togetherness leave fairness to God and go to him for the satisfaction you would get from justice. Your family will notice.

At family gatherings it's easy to feel unappreciated, especially for those who are wired to serve. Serving can be done physically, by helping with preparation and cleanup, or spiritually and emotionally, by listening, caring, and biting your tongue. You can feel like everyone is having a good time while you do all the work, and no one notices or seems to care. Even though you're motivated to serve without anyone asking, it's still hard to release expectations of a little bit of credit or reciprocation. This might help: tell God you want to do good and serve your family, and you do *not* want anyone to say thank you for it. You're asking God to keep it between him and you. Now you're ready to be unappreciated, and you'll thank God for it. God humbled himself and came to earth as a lowly human, born as a baby in poverty and humility. He deserved worship but received rejection and punishment. You'll be in good company.

Drops of Grace for the Estranged or Barely Talking Family

How do you influence when you rarely connect? Maybe you still get together occasionally, but in between there's not much contact. You would like more contact, if it can be good contact.

Start small. Lower your expectations. Let other families go to the moon. You just walk down the sidewalk a few feet. Baby steps. Little things.

Think brief, small, but purposeful touches. Think generosity and giving.

Think honesty. Encouragement. Praise.

Call or text something short. Yes, you'd be going against the grain and taking the initiative. The reaction will probably be, *What's this about? They never do this.* Since it's so surprising and attention-getting, you don't need to do much. The message itself is the surprising touch. Make it an "I was just thinking of you, thought I'd say hi" kind of thing. With a text, keep it light with emoticons. Then do it again in a few days or weeks. Over time make short, positive touches a normal thing.

> *Find one true, positive, unique, good thing about a member of your family whom you want to touch. Then tell them that one thing.*

Stay away from the past, from controversy, and from drama. You're not denying problems exist; you're just covering them over with love for now.

Find one true, positive, unique, good thing about a member of your family whom you want to touch. Then tell them that one thing. Again, call, text, or email. In-person is even better if possible. Keep it short with no big discussions. Short leaves less time for misinterpretation or for things to go wrong. "You know, you really look great . . . do that well . . . take care of things around here . . . make an awesome meat loaf . . ." Or "I love the way you _____." But again, it has to be true.

Find one true thing, then another, then another. You can't start a fire without a spark. Then you need some kindling. You add bigger logs later. If you had to make one true, good comment to a family member right now, what would it be and to whom?

Habits of Drops of Grace—for Those Who Like a Method

Common, good advice from financial advisers is to save money by paying yourself first. The idea is to make the deposit into savings happen automatically, so you don't need to remind or discipline yourself to do it, which makes it more likely to occur. Once the account is set up, your savings build up over time.

You can do the same thing with drops of grace, if you make certain drops for certain people happen automatically. Of course, you don't want to make saying "I love you" an automatic habit, but the habit of giving some small drop of grace can build momentum.

BJ Fogg is a behavior scientist at Stanford University. He majors in habits and how behavior changes. He uses a method called Tiny Habits.[3] You could try his method to develop the habit of drops of grace.

He says only three things change behavior:

1. An epiphany
2. A change of environment
3. Baby steps

Since we can't control epiphany, and changing your environment might not be an option, we'll focus on baby steps.

The whole trick with baby steps is to make them so small that you hardly have to try, so small that you don't need willpower. Fogg says this is the key to making new habits. Baby steps will cut down on your natural resistance to change and doing something new. In fact, make it such a ridiculously small step that you're sure it won't work. Dr. Fogg says it will.

Think of what you'd like to see or feel in your family, then think of a small starter step toward that, a small drop of grace that you'd like to establish. Small means something you can do in less than thirty seconds, that requires little effort, that's painless and easy, and that requires no willpower—a small bit of grace to drop in the river where your family is now.

You're going to cooperate with how God has already designed family to be contagious. You're going to take advantage of his design and trust that those drops will spread over time, which they will because behavior is contagious.

If you want, Professor Fogg says a powerful key is to attach your tiny habit—your drops of grace—to something that already happens every day. It could be eating breakfast, brushing your teeth, or preparing for bed—anchor it to anything you already do automatically. You could think of it this way: *After I* _____ (current habit), *I will* _____ (new drops of grace habit).

To start, think of two bits of grace you'd like to drop, and do them at least once every day for five days. Each time you do them, celebrate with a fist pump, "Yes!," or "Thank you, Lord." Professor Fogg says the little celebration is important because we're wired to thrive on encouragement. Since you're modeling grace for your family and it's going to be contagious, isn't that worth celebrating?

Following is a summary of the Tiny Habits method:

Pick a small drop of grace that you'd like to see touch your family.

To start the habit, make it small and simple—a drop of grace the size of a mustard seed. Once it's a habit you can make it bigger.

To make it simple and easy, anchor that drop to something that already happens every day.

Every time you do it, celebrate so that you feel successful.

Here's what it looked like the first time I tried this method:

1. When I leave the bedroom in the morning, I will kiss Brenda on the forehead (I usually get up before she does).
2. Whenever I come home, I'll ask Brenda, "What one thing can I do for you?"

Other ideas:

After I _____, I will text a heart to _____ (that's all—texting is awesome for little drops of grace).

After I _____, I will give one sincere compliment (you have to think of one and be ready).

More possible drops of grace habits:

- Hold hands with someone and pray for thirty seconds and thank God for that person.
- Ask, "How are you feeling?" then smile and listen.
- Ask, "How can I help you?" and mean it.
- Count to five before responding to offenses.
- Ask, "How could I have made your day better today?"
- Pick up, put away, throw away _____.
- Text some inside phrase/code word (mine is "warm thoughts").
- Text anything clearly meaningful to that person.
- Say, "I love it when you _____."
- Write a note on a Post-it note and post it.
- Write a short email: "Just want you to know I appreciate you."
- Keep a stash of _____ and give one with no comment.

What are your ideas? Make the first week about practicing. Keep the gesture small and foolproof, so small you don't think it will make a difference. Then watch what happens.

A Few More Drops of Grace

The following are a few more ideas to do with a family member or your family as a whole:

- Learn their love language.
- Do small things for them in their love language.
- Find something to do together that helps someone else.
- Do an extra thing, step, or favor beyond what's expected.
- Take a Myers-Briggs Type Indicator personality test together and talk about the results.
- Ask for their help with something. They'll feel valuable and connect it to you.
- Develop code words and phrases in your relationship—my sister and I end every call with "I love you and I'm glad you're my sister/brother."
- Ask, "What is one thing you would change about me?"
- Say, "You can do it." (Saying this may seem wimpy to most of us, but for those who have never heard these words, they can be powerful.)
- Say, "So you're saying _____," and summarize in your own words what you think they're saying, so they know that you understand.
- Say, "I'm sorry. I was wrong and you were right."
- Say, "It's OK, no big deal."

And the most powerful, frightening question that can result in a deluge of drops of grace from you for someone else: Ask yourself, "What is it like to live with me?"

By the way, I know that many of these suggestions may seem simplistic and even laughable, but I offer them without apology. If you say to me, "These are so cheesy and would never do any good in my family," I would respond with, "I know, so please come up with your own ideas to fit what your family needs." That's the goal, for you to drip your own drops of grace into your own family river.

If you've had a certain family member in mind as you've read to this point, a person who rubs you the wrong way, whose relationship is challenging, then good news—the next chapter offers a chance to take one big step in that relationship.

— 14 —

One Big Step in Your Most Challenging Family Relationship

Charting Your Course

> The longer you've known someone—the more history there is between you—the longer it will take to establish in their mind that you have truly changed.
>
> Andy Andrews

No one is exempt or immune from challenging family relationships. Jesus Christ was misunderstood, unappreciated, and even rejected by his family. Family relationships are uniquely challenging because they are so everyday, so constant, so close, so familiar. You're always exposed to each other or working hard to hide from each other—either way you can't avoid each other. The challenge can go on for so long that we resign ourselves to it. We don't feel there's anything we can do to make things better, and the pressure becomes so familiar that it feels normal.

This chapter takes everywhere we've been in this book so far and presents a simple blueprint for a way to navigate one of the rapids in your family river. You'll learn some actions to take and some words to say to try to find relief in your most challenging family relationship. There are many blueprints you could use—this is just one example. Once you try it, you may think of other ideas or ways to adapt it to fit your situation.

> *Let's be grateful that there's at least one thing we have control over—ourselves, with God's help—and that our influence is powerful.*

This may or may not be for you. Some people want a plan and specific steps of action; others want only to be given the destination and then pointed in the right direction. Even if you're one of the latter, you may still benefit from seeing how the pieces can fit together, and there may be one thing that lights up for you.

If you jump in here without reading what came before, you will probably have a lot of questions. You could easily think, *Wait a minute, I'm the one who has to take the initiative? I'm the one who needs to be selfless, as if the problem is all me? Well, it's not all me; in fact, it's mostly them. But I'm the one doing all the work?* My response to those feelings is in the chapters leading up to this point. For now, you are the one reading this, not them. I can't talk to them, only you. Let's be grateful that there's at least one thing we have control over—ourselves, with God's help—and that our influence is powerful.

With Whom Is Your Most Challenging Relationship?

When we first began, you had an opportunity to select one or two people to keep in mind as you proceeded. Now you have a chance to take a few specific steps with those one or two people.

Maybe it's your spouse. There are many helpful marriage resources—books, retreats, conferences, and counseling—but even the decision about which resource to use is complicated. In the end, few do anything. This is something simple to try.

Maybe it's friction between mother-in-law and daughter-in-law.

Maybe it's conflict between parents and adult children over expectations and life choices. The kids want to live their own lives, without a guilt trip. The parents know from experience what works. You both just want to be heard and respected.

Maybe it's one of the younger ones still at home, or more than one, or all of them!

Maybe the adult siblings are disconnected, angry, and even estranged.

Maybe it's you, feeling ignored, disrespected, marginalized by almost everyone.

Maybe it's your grown daughter. You feel her heart slipping away, and you long to reclaim it before it's too late. Or you're the grown daughter, and you feel distant from your mom or dad. Or maybe it's clashes with a grown son.

Maybe it's that person who is just hard to live with and hard to love. Or maybe you're concerned about what's happening with a loved one—they seem troubled and you can't break through, and it pains you.

I'll present a simple plan to follow that can reduce the pain and disappointment and increase your joy and peace. It could result in your most challenging family relationship being changed forever. It could help every family relationship you have.

I'm going to offer you three laws that you can trust and believe. Like all laws, when you cooperate with them, things go well. Then we'll look at three paths that you can take, and because of the three laws that you can trust, you can be confident that these three paths will make a difference.

You do *not* need to take what you learn here and change everything you're doing. You just need to see a few things to try, discover what might make a difference, then try it. Or you may be inspired to come up with your own ideas. Whatever you do, you will begin to feel some relief, connection, even peace and joy, in your most challenging family relationship.

Your Attitudes and Expectations Shape Your Family

Change your attitudes and expectations, and your family changes. Your perspective influences what you say and do and how you feel. You can change how you look at relationships and try new things,

> *Change your attitudes and expectations, and your family changes.*

and I know what a lot of those new things are because I've been down the same road and have come out the other side. And I took notes for all of us.

And here's what my notes say: start with a basic, simple blueprint and build on that. It will take some time, but you're way ahead of where I was when I started back in the "how can I make my family happy" days. You've already gone through the clueless-lost-in-the-jungle years, so let's take a big step into a happier place.

Three Laws to Trust

We trust and obey laws all the time, following them without even thinking about them. Laws give us a starting place, so we don't need to figure everything out from scratch. When I drive through a new area, I don't need to evaluate it and calculate what a reasonable speed would be. I only need to look at the speed limit sign. If I cooperate with the posted speed, things should turn out fine. Much of life works this way.

You can trust that you can cook fish about ten minutes per inch of thickness. It's like a law. When cooking pork, you know it's safe to eat when the internal temperature gets to about 145 degrees. Another law.

Other areas of life have "laws" too. If you raise your voice and argue, the other person probably will too. In general, dark colors make you look slimmer, light colors make you look heavier. Drink coffee at 10:00 p.m. and you'll probably have trouble sleeping. Drink it in the morning and it will help you wake up and be alert. I don't have to wonder what effect drinking coffee will have—I just need to know the "coffee law."

The wisest man who ever lived (apart from Jesus) paid close attention to people's behavior and to the "laws" that governed consequences.

> Whoever brings blessing will be enriched, and one who waters will himself be watered. (Prov. 11:25)

> Whoever covers an offense seeks love. (Prov. 17:9)

> A soft tongue will break a bone. (Prov. 25:15)

> A soft answer turns away wrath, but a harsh word stirs up anger. (Prov. 15:1)

> The purpose in a man's heart is like deep water, but a man of understanding will draw it out. (Prov. 20:5)

For our purposes here, when I say "law," I don't mean as in "you must do this." I mean, like A leads to B, you can be confident of predicting the consequences. The following three laws will all be familiar to you, since I've mentioned them in some form earlier. As we go through them, picture the family relationship that is so challenging to you. Picture that person. Then picture these three laws in effect in your relationship. Afterward, we'll look at ways to cooperate with them.

Law #1: Words, Actions, Attitudes, and Emotions Are Contagious

Families are designed for influence, and you're always influencing someone whether you are trying to or not.

Every family has a unique personality because the members influence each other. When you *try* to influence, the design automatically helps you. You can take advantage of this by modeling what you want others to "catch."

Law #2: When People Feel You Care, They Soften Toward You

When you help people feel accepted, cared about, heard, and understood, it causes them to feel valued and appreciated, to soften, to calm down, and to open up to you.

They lose the urgency to prove themselves and be right. Their self-protective exterior softens. They can afford to be generous and unselfish. They feel good, and they connect feeling good with you.

It's hard to have a negative, challenging family relationship with someone who's calm, soft, generous, unselfish, and who trusts you. Caring about them affects their feelings toward you; they trust you. Then those feelings can turn into a loop of caring and trusting between you.

If you want people to soften and open up to you, help them feel good about themselves and show that you want good for them.

Law #3: When You See into a Person's Heart, You Soften Toward Them

This goes both ways—when you see into someone's heart, you soften toward them; when they see into your heart, they soften toward you.

When you begin to understand someone's heart, how they really feel, hear their heartbeat, see some of their story, it causes your heart to go out to them. It affects your feelings toward them.

If you want to soften toward others, get to know them better. People who want to fight or be angry with someone can't let themselves get to know their adversary. If you begin to understand why they do what they do that makes you so angry, you won't be able to fight them or hate them any longer.

When you see a person demonizing someone, stereotyping, seeing someone as all bad, these actions indicate that they want to stay angry at that person and that they choose not to see any good in them. This says more about the demonizer than the demonized.

> *If you want to soften toward others, get to know them better.*

See Where You're Going in Your One Big Step?

You're moving toward softening your most challenging family relationship. Would it be a big step if you could feel them soften toward you, and you toward them, and if you could feel like they cared for you, and you for them? Even if your relationship softens only a little bit, wouldn't that bring some relief?

So already we can see that if these three laws are true, then they provide a simple beginning. And they are true. Remember, I've been on both sides of these laws—the side where I respond emotionally and with my limited perspective, and the side where I cooperate with the way God has created us to relate to each other. I've seen both sides for forty-five years, and I've paid attention—and these three laws are true.

And since these three laws are true, let's keep it simple and just start here.

I'm not asking you to commit to the laws. I'm only asking if you can accept for now that they're true. If that's too difficult, then do this—just for now, pretend that you believe these three laws are true. That will work fine too. Your challenging family relationship is going to get much simpler.

When you trust and believe these things, they become an awesome relational soup stock. Everything good begins here. Since we're accepting these laws, our assignment has become simpler: cooperate and trust, and let the laws God created do their work.

Our assignment is simple because there are only three ways we relate to people within our families. In those three ways, we just cooperate with these three laws. What are those three ways we relate to people? Those are the paths we talked about. Like I've been saying, three laws to trust and three paths to take.

We've seen the three laws. They are:

1. Words, actions, attitudes, and emotions are contagious.

2. When people feel you care, they soften toward you.

3. When you see into a person's heart, *you* soften toward *them*.

Now let's look at the three paths.

Three Paths to Take

There's the path of what we *say*, the path of what we *do*, and the path of what we *think*, which includes our attitudes, assumptions, expectations, and motives.

That's all there is, right? That's how you relate to people. It can't get much simpler than that.

You say things to someone.

You do things for them, to them, and with them.

And you think things in your head—you have attitudes, expectations, and opinions.

There's nothing else but these paths of relating to each other. We all know this intuitively, but we don't think of relationships as being that simple. They are.

And if the things you say and do and think are cooperating with the three laws—taking advantage of the three laws—then you *are* going to find relief in your most challenging family relationship. How much relief and how quickly it happens depend on a number of things. But if you take those three laws and from them decide what to say, what to do, and what to think, your most challenging family relationship will get better.

You don't have to follow all three paths perfectly. You don't even have to follow all three paths at once—one or two will make a difference. Likewise, you don't have to follow all three laws at once—one or two will make a difference. Anything you do in any of the three paths that cooperates with any of the three laws is going to make a difference.

You can learn as you go. Maybe start with one path and one law. Just do some things there, and you'll begin to find relief in your most challenging family relationship. But the more laws and paths you follow, the bigger the step you take and the better it will be.

Path #1: What to Say

When you speak, you want to cooperate with the three laws, which means: words are contagious. So say things that you want to spread.

When they feel you care, they'll soften toward you. So say things that will show them you care.

When you see their heart, you'll soften toward them. So say things that will help you know them better and help you see their heart.

But what *kinds* of words? What are the actual words you should say?

> *What if I told you there is a secret list of powerful, relationship-changing words that can forever change your most challenging family relationship?*

What if I told you there is a secret list of powerful, relationship-changing words that can forever change your most challenging family relationship?

That would be a bold claim to make. I don't want to make that claim. It seems too much like an exaggerated marketing ploy. But I believe that it's true. There is such a list. You've never seen that list, but we're going to begin to access it right now.

Picture the person in your most challenging family relationship and think, *What words or phrases would I like to hear from them?*

"I'm sorry."

"You're right."

"I don't know what's gotten into me."

You might like to hear words like that, right? What else? What other kinds of words and phrases would you like to hear from them *if your relationship was what you wanted it to be*? When you did the Family Satisfaction Assessment and the What I Want to See list, you had a chance to write down a brief description of what you'd like to see and feel in your most challenging family relationships. You could remind yourself of that now, or just think of words or phrases you'd like to hear from that person who is so challenging to you. What kinds of words from them would give you relief in your challenging relationship? Can you write a few of them down? I'll bet you'd like to hear

a sincere compliment

appreciation

that they need your help or want your advice

that you matter to them

that they've noticed what you've done for them

them brag on you to someone else

We're not talking about long, sit-down conversations, just phrases during normal as-you-go conversations. Some of those phrases would be lighthearted humor that feels like little drops of grace, and when you hear them more than once, they begin to add up for you.

This is your unique relationship, and only you know the words that would give you some relief and satisfaction in this relationship. You want your own list of words and phrases. Be overly hopeful when you make your list. Don't think, *Oh, they'd never say that.* If you'd like to hear it, write it down.

Finish your list. Now look it over. If you heard those words and phrases, how would they make you feel about that person? Write it down.

Now we go radical. What if those same words from you would make the individual in your most challenging family relationship feel the same way? And what if they feel *toward you* the way you feel *toward them* when you imagine them saying those words?

What if you then were reminded of the three laws?

1. Words, actions, attitudes, and emotions are contagious.
2. When people feel you care, they soften toward you.
3. When you see into a person's heart, *you* soften toward *them.*

If you know that what you say is contagious and that caring can make them soften toward you, what does that make you want to say to them?

Look again at your list and ask yourself, *Which of these words would be appropriate for me to say to them?* Your list began with what you would like to hear. Now you're using that list to discern what they would like to hear.

Some items might not fit. But some—maybe many—will be perfect, and powerful, coming from you. Which ones?

You have now discovered the secret list of powerful, relationship-changing words that can forever change your most challenging family relationship. And it's personalized for you. The question is, what will you do with this list now that you have it?

In the days of Elisha, Naaman was told Elisha could cure his leprosy, but when Elisha sent his servant out with a message to Naaman to go wash himself in the Jordan seven times, Namaan became angry. The answer was too plain and simple. He expected a dramatic, impressive solution from Elisha personally, something worthy of Naaman's status and the wealth he was willing to pay. But it was God's solution, not Elisha's. Namaan wanted to dictate the answer to his problem.

> If what you say has value, it will last longer than you will.
>
> Vance Havner[1]

Are you willing to trust God and simply wash in the Jordan by trying these very personal words and phrases you've discovered? Following are more suggestions for you to use. Though not as targeted to your own relationship as the words and phrases on your personal list, some might be perfect for you. You can pick any of these to add to your list or use them as idea starters for more of your own phrases.

"How can I make your day better today?"
"What are you encouraged about right now?"
"What do you feel most challenged about right now?"
"What would a perfect day look like for you?"
"If you could change one thing about me, what would it be?"
"I love it/appreciate it when you . . ."
Brag and talk positively about them in front of someone.
Tell them you bragged about them to someone else.
Give a sincere compliment or express appreciation, with no strings: "You know what I appreciate about you . . . ?"
What words show you're interested in them as a person?
Follow up something they say by being curious and attentive.

When they share something that's going on, maybe a challenge or an opportunity, you can connect by asking questions that show you care and that help you see inside them:

"How does that _____ make you feel?"

"Tell me more about that . . ."

"What do you think that means?"

"What do you think God is doing with that?"

"If this could turn out the way you want, what would it look like?"

It's also possible your relationship is not the kind in which any of these would fit or make sense; if so, move on and accept the uniqueness of your relationship and allow the Lord to show you personally how to walk with him in it.

Path #2: What to Do

In all three paths—what to say, what to do, what to think— you're following what seems to be a simple law of the universe, the eternal law of reciprocation: with the measure you use, it will be measured to you.

> Love your enemies, and do good, and lend, expecting nothing in return, and your reward will be great, and you will be sons of the Most High, for he is kind to the ungrateful and the evil. Be merciful, even as your Father is merciful.
>
> Judge not, and you will not be judged; condemn not, and you will not be condemned; forgive, and you will be forgiven; give, and it will be given to you. Good measure, pressed down, shaken together, running over, will be put into your lap. For with the measure you use it will be measured back to you. (Luke 6:35–38)

This reciprocation "law" is important enough that Jesus refers to it in Matthew 7 as well: "With the judgment you pronounce you will be judged, and with the measure you use it will be measured to you" (v. 2).

The law of reciprocation with regard to love, judgment, forgiveness, and generosity seems to apply *at least* to enemies, all of which relates to your challenging family relationship. Therefore,

201

be confident of the influence you have in this relationship and of the real possibility of relief and satisfaction.

The first path is what to *say*.

Now we're going to consider the second path, what to *do*, in terms of the three laws and the law of reciprocation. Some people are more sensitive to actions than words. Maybe you're more a doer than a sayer, so you may prefer this path.

Think again of that person in your most challenging family relationship. What would you like that person to do for you or with you or to you?

What actions of theirs would give you relief in your relationship? What actions would make you feel valued, make you soften toward them? Go through the same process you did with path #1, only this time in regard to actions.

I'll bet if that person looked you in the eye and gave you a genuine smile, you'd like that. You might even respond in kind. Depending on your relationship, that might be real relief to you.

What if you got a text from them for no reason, just saying, "Hey, I was thinking of you"?

What if, in return for saying something somewhat harsh and realizing it too late, you received a positive reaction, maybe even a little smile?

What if you began to notice they were letting little offenses go without responding in kind? As if the offenses didn't happen?

What if they knew your love language and—on purpose—did something for you in your language?

Or what if they left you a bag of Ghirardelli caramel squares with a sticky note with your name on it? (Or insert your own favorite indulgence.)

This is your relationship. I'm just trying to get you thinking. This needs to be your own list. Dream of this relationship being what you want it to be—what could they do for you, with you, or to you that would make you feel good, or relieved, or closer to them? Write it down.

Do the same thing with this path that you did with path #1. Take a minute to look over your list. If the person in your challenging relationship did these things, how would it make you feel toward them?

Write down how it would make you feel.

Now, what if those same actions *from you* would make them feel the same way? And what if those same actions would make them feel the same way *toward you* that you feel toward them when you imagine them doing them? "Whatever you wish that others would do to you, do also to them" (Matt. 7:12).

What if you again were reminded of the three laws?

1. Words, actions, attitudes, and emotions are contagious.

2. When people feel you care, they soften toward you.

3. When you see into a person's heart, *you* soften toward *them*.

What action do these laws make you want to take? If you know these three things will happen, what do they make you want to do to that person, or for them, or with them?

Look again at your list and ask yourself, *Which of these actions would be appropriate for me to do to them?*

You have now discovered another secret list, this one of powerful, relationship-changing actions that can forever change your most challenging family relationship. And it's personalized for you. The question is, what will you do with this list now that you have it?

Path #3: What to Think

If you've gone down the two previous paths, then you are catching on to how to personally apply "whatever you wish others would do to you, do also to them." Do the same thing you did for what to do and what to say.

What would you like them to think about you? What would you like them to assume about you?

One of the most common problems in relationships is how easy it is to believe someone else thinks negatively of us, and how easy it is to be convinced that they think things of us that aren't true.

So what would you like them to think?

I assume you'd like them to think positively about you and be sensitive to your attitudes and moods. You'd like for them to give you the benefit of the doubt.

What are those thoughts and attitudes? What would you like them to assume about you? Be hopeful. Write it down.

Look at your list. How does it make you feel?

What if it would make them feel the same way if *you* thought those things and had those attitudes about *them*?

Which of those thoughts and attitudes could you honestly have toward them? Find true things, or at least find areas where you can give them the benefit of the doubt.

Now you have another secret list, this one of powerful, relationship-changing thoughts and attitudes that can forever change your most challenging family relationship. The question is, what will you do with this list?

By faith, little by little, can you adopt a few of these gracious thoughts, attitudes, and assumptions toward them? Expect that somehow over time the measure you use will be measured back to you.

Start Small and Start Now

This one-big-step process is one example of applying everything you've read in this book. You don't need to do all of it. You can pick the easiest path and law to start with. Try just a few new words or actions or attitudes in your relationship.

Perhaps you've been inspired in some other way, maybe to combine this method with some other idea or exercise. Whatever it is, walk that way. My discovery of the *Timeless Tools* began small and slow, and then grew and multiplied over time—but I had to begin.

Remember how the Mississippi River begins? A stream babbling over rocks as it leaves a small lake and heads north—north?—looking nothing like where it ends up twenty-five hundred miles later. Over time it turns south and slowly begins to respond to God's wooing to become great. Right now you might feel like one of the tourists standing on those rocks at the source of the Mississippi, hardly getting their feet wet, hardly able to imagine the path the river takes to become what God has in mind.

That process can begin right now for you, and you can step confidently into the river knowing where it's going. You might head north for a while, but in the end there's a bay, and a dock, and a time of appreciation and gratitude for the journey you were privileged to be a part of.

— 15 —

Dock of the Bay

Resting in Your Legacy of Grace

Family is a verb, family is an action that we choose
because family is not just what we are, it's something
that we keep on actively making. Turns out it's not only
the blood in our veins that makes us family—it's the
blood and sacrifice in our days that makes us family.

Ann Voskamp

Whenever we leave church or a movie or any kind of get-together,
I always ask Brenda for her observations, what she took away
from the experience. I'd ask you that same question now, but, of
course, I can't.

You have your own personal takeaways. However, if you asked
me what takeaways I'd wish for you, these would be the words.

Though Proverbs reminds us that "whoever covers over an offense seeks love" (17:9), one obstacle stands atop the mountain

206

of family discontent—a cursed colossus that is the mega block to family harmony, the one single thing that, if changed, could have the biggest effect on a family's ability to get along.

What is this pillar of pain?

Bitterness. It comes from keeping score.

When we see a news story about a family member who attacks another family member over the TV remote or macaroni and cheese, we all know it's not about the remote or the mac and cheese. It's about everything that's happened before that. Those things add up because we keep score. We think we are more hurt, more offended, and more wrongly accused.

When I think you owe me more than I owe you, I feel resentment toward you. I don't want to call it a grudge, but that's what it is. I have a big chip on my shoulder. But I handle it like I think a Christian should, which to me means being nice on the outside and not overtly paying you back what I think you deserve.

Instead, I pay you back *covertly*. My heart is cool toward you. I suspect a negative motive in almost everything you do and say. I don't trust you. I never ask you a personal or caring question. And here's the worst part that I will *never* admit to—it feels a little sweet, in a strangely perverted way, to be so offended and bugged by you. It feels kind of good to be owed.

The Big Blind Spot

I can't possibly comprehend that you feel the same toward me. The bitterness, the chip on your shoulder, the cool heart, the martyrdom of smiling on the outside, the sweetness of being owed big time—all that goes both ways?

That is outrageous and maddening to me. And I am even more offended. How dare you think it's me! Sure, I hold some blame, but nothing like you. No way. Ridiculous.

And, of course, you feel the same way.

And thus we have tormented marriages, families, and extended family relationships. You become the one I can hardly talk about. My nemesis. And I become yours.

How long can this go on? What if this situation doesn't change? What is the cost to you? What is the cost to the other person? What's going to happen if it doesn't change?

I'm sixty-five years old, and I've seen what will happen.

Years will go by. I wish I could go back thirty years to Tommy (remember the boxer?) and Carolyn's home at Thanksgiving. Everyone was together, everyone was married, everyone was alive. The kids were growing up. The day was noisy, crowded, and fun. Those were wonderful holidays with Brenda's family. Yes, there were disagreements and dysfunction, but hey, there was time to work through that.

I thought those days would last forever. I thought we had time to fix anything that needed fixing. But time, like family, is a river—it flows on and doesn't stop—and it takes everything and everybody with it. Your challenging relationships just keep repeating the same scenes, and you keep going the same way with that person you can hardly talk to or about, your nemesis.

You may ask—I've asked—*Can life keep going like this forever?* I used to ask that about my dad, and I learned, yes, it can, and it can even get worse. Rarely do things get better on their own.

You just keep getting older, and so do they. I hate having to remind you of this. After decades of marriage, two people end up strangers. Grown kids or your mother-in-law or daughter-in-law move away, and you lose contact. The disconnect becomes normal, and you learn to live with it.

Then come other things that happen over the years in families—health problems, estrangement, divorce. And then you're at the end of your life, and they're at the end of theirs, and it makes you sick thinking about that relationship that was never mended. And people think, *It's just too late.*

NO, We're Not Going to Let That Happen!

Life is for living and enjoying. Family relationships should be fulfilling, and as you've discovered, your family is already designed to bring about that fullness for each of you. Of course, there are problems and dysfunctions along the way—but they don't need to dominate and rule your relationships.

Just by reading this far you've already said no to that sad future depiction. It took me twenty years to learn that I can influence people and situations by what I think and say and do. You have already taken that big step. By reading this you are rejecting hopelessness and complacency. You are saying, "This family is worth it! These relationships are valuable and powerful!" And you're saying, "If this particular relationship is powerful enough to make me feel challenged and stressed, then it's powerful enough to give me satisfaction and joy."

People who say what you're saying make a difference.

> "If this particular relationship is powerful enough to make me feel challenged and stressed, then it's powerful enough to give me satisfaction and joy."

I feel I already know you. You've been willing to do and try things, but you haven't known what to do and try. You've wanted to know how to think and what to do so you could make things better. And now you know some of those things. You don't just want to wish and hope. You're a person who accepts responsibility for your actions, for your relationships, and for yourself.

You're not an excuse maker, a victim, a blamer. You're not a complainer or a person who just expects the other person to change.

You wanted a little guidance paddling the rapids, and you got it. You're not lost anymore; you know what's healthy and what's not in your family relationships. You've found someone to help you discover what is best for you and your family. You've received

some realistic, understandable, and practical step-by-step suggestions from someone who has been there. You've seen examples of
what to do and what not to do. No, the information is not custom-
tailored for you and your family; no book can do that. But *you*
can do what's best for your family with what you've been given
here. "In humility count others more significant than" yourself
(Phil. 2:3).

We all know that family has the greatest potential for joy and
peace, and it has the greatest potential for pain and disappointment. We're going to get more joy and peace!

In Deuteronomy 30, God said that the life he wanted for the
people he loved was not too hard for them, it was not far off, it
was not in heaven or beyond the sea where someone needed to go
get it. He said it was actually already very near them so they could
do it. It's the same for you—you already knew much of this, the
attitudes and perspectives and kinds of actions that make things
better. But you either didn't believe in them or didn't realize how
powerful those things can be.

Now you know. Now you see how the things you've known are
actually real tools that can make every family relationship better.
Up to now you've used the tools haphazardly without realizing
how powerful and interrelated they are and what the results can
be. But now you know. I hope you feel encouraged.

When We Began

When we began way back in the morning sun with that conversation at Panera, I said, "You'll look back and know you didn't just
survive, you didn't just provide nurture and direction; you deeply
influenced the people God created them to be. And in doing that,
you influenced all the people they influence, now and later. You
will have dented the world with grace. All because of your family.
You'll feel better, even about the one you can't talk about."

You've taken a big step. You're already closer to that peaceful rest when the evening comes, knowing you have deeply affected for good your family legacy.

Maybe you began with that default in all of us that says it's all about results. We want things to be different, and the easiest way to get results seems to be the direct way of telling, pushing, correcting, and scolding. We could call that "the Hand." Sometimes that method seems to work, but for some reason we need to keep repeating it. The Hand just wants to get things done.

> The thing that tells in the long run for God and for men, is the steady persevering work in the unseen.
>
> Oswald Chambers[1]

We learn a better way is the way of "the Head," where we realize the value of persuasion and convincing. The Head gets the other person to buy into a direction or decision. So much better! We're in agreement!

But something is missing. If you've ever disappointed your parents or spouse or kids *so much* that you were grieved and so were they, then you understand a bit about what's missing with the Hand and the Head. What's missing is "the Heart."

The Hand cares mostly about results. Just get it done.

The Head cares mostly about persuasion and convincing. Results matter, but the Head wants you to want to.

The Heart cares mostly about your relationship.

With the Heart, results might not be worth it if getting there comes between you and the other person. When you get to this place, you are at, as Oswald Chambers says, the utmost. You're becoming one with Jesus's desire for his presence in you to connect with his presence in the other person or in your family.

What would it take to have the kind of relationship with someone that made both of you not want to do anything that hindered that relationship? A relationship in which a lack of results is not as painful as a lack of companionship?

If you have anything close to that kind of relationship with even one person, you know the kinds of things it takes to maintain that relationship and make it grow—things such as acceptance, grace, patience, caring, generosity, commitment, encouragement, and humor.

You're becoming one with Jesus's desire for his presence in you to connect with his presence in the other person or in your family.

When you make the relationship the most important thing, guess what happens? As a by-product, you get the results you desired when you tried the Hand or the Head. Or maybe it just seems that way. Maybe the relationship changes the results you want. Either way, slowly over time the heart connection grows, like a romance, until there's something special between you that becomes more important than anything else.

That's how it's worked for Brenda and me. I may have a preference for which house we buy, but that preference weighs far less than my desire for her to be happy. And my desire for her happiness doesn't come from some painful sacrifice. We've been together a long time, and I love her so much that my happiness has merged with hers.

Sometimes helping her be happy feels so good it feels selfish. Not always, of course, but our relationship is characterized by that kind of thing. And she feels the same way. You might think this is a result of forty years of work, but for the first twenty years we were clueless and went in the hole of selfish negativity trying to influence each other with the Hand.

In God there is no hunger that needs to be filled, only plenteousness that desires to give.

C. S. Lewis[2]

Ten years later, we were out of the hole and on our way to a decent level of unselfishness with the Head and more of the Heart.

Growing takes time but not forever. If you're in the hole, you can get out. Soon your family could be fighting over insisting the other person gets their way. If you start now.

A Family like Yours

If you start now, you can end up with a family characterized by harmony and unity, therefore, "as God's chosen people, holy and dearly loved, clothe yourselves with compassion, kindness, humility, gentleness, and patience" (Col. 3:12). Bitterness and anger may still flare up, but they won't dominate.

> Forgiveness is the fragrance of the violet on the heel of the one who has crushed it.
>
> George Roemisch[3]

You'll end up with a family of grace-filled individuals. Or maybe just one individual. One individual—you—who realizes you might be wrong.

Who doesn't insist on fairness, even in your inward thoughts.

Who refuses to keep score.

Who notices your own offenses more than those of others.

Who knows by experience the negative consequences of a rash, loud response, and who now practices patient, quiet responses.

Who'd rather give in when you're right than win when you're wrong.

Who'd rather trust a person's motives when you shouldn't than not trust their motives when you should.

Who's confident that giving grace is contagious in a family and whose confidence and grace spread.

Who trusts that this one thing—in humility refusing to keep score—kills the seed of bitterness and creates a growing garden of grace in your family.

And who's grateful that today is another day to nurture that garden.

Welcome, friend, to walking with Jesus in your family.

Acknowledgments

We introverts can be supremely content as loners, but it's not always good for us. It's also not good for the people we want to help and influence. Sure, you write by yourself, but for writing to be as good as it can be and get to the people you wrote for, you need help.

This book is about going from cluelessness to enlightenment, and my publishing journey has traveled the same path. Helen Keller said, "Walking with a friend in the dark is better than walking alone in the light."[1] I'm grateful for the helpful friends who have walked with me.

Myquillyn and Emily helped when they said, "Dad, you should write about family." What a blessing to have grown daughters always rooting for me and always seeing the best in me.

Andrea Doering helped when she said, "This could be a book," after reading one of those things I wrote about family. She was a writer's dream come true: she came to me for a book; then she shepherded it through the acquisitions process at Revell and became the super encourager and editor of the book.

Esther Fedorkevich helped when she said, "I'd love to be your agent—then I'd represent your whole family!" Then she worked the magic for which she's known.

Whitney Gossett and Lauren Hall—also with the Fedd Agency—helped tremendously with the proposal and talking through promotions and endorsements.

My wife, Brenda, helped when she read the manuscript chapter by chapter. I kept waiting for her to say something negative or corrective. Finally, she said, "We need to talk about this chapter." I knew she'd tell me the truth about parts that didn't work, so her approval meant even more. I actually loved it when she got tough. She's a big reader and knows bad writing and thinking when she sees it. BTW, that chapter's not in the book.

My daughter Emily has published four books with Revell and has always been positive about her relationships and experiences with them. So connecting with Revell was comforting for a first-time author, like meeting old friends. Twila Bennett helped with marketing and publicity and a title and a cover and lots of encouragement. Cheryl Van Andel and Andy Vaubel helped by creating the cover. Emily Uebbing, Erin Bartels, and Wendy Wetzel helped with questions and details that shaped the book throughout the process.

Gisèle Mix with Revell was graciously encouraging and helped refine the ideas and details. Melinda Timmer and Amy Nemecek helped as proofreaders to catch the little pieces that are always missed no matter how many stages our writing goes through. Patti Brinks and Dan Malda helped by designing the beautiful and inviting cover and pages you've been reading. Thank you!

The Hopewriters.com community, the most encouraging, positive, helpful group of writers in the world—and too many to name—gave invaluable help with clarity on the title. Brian Dixon with Hope*writers helped by always pushing to focus on the reader.

It's a scary thing to write in private and then turn your writing loose into a wild, unpredictable world. I'm super grateful for a group of first reader friends who read an early version of the book to help me clarify things that might be confusing or distracting to a broad audience: Brian and Starr Haigler, Ken DeLamater, Melissa Prince, Mary Cioffi, Barney Quick, Traci Hardy, Joe Paulo, Daniel Arroyo, Ashley Sehoff, Donna Chiavoli, Maria Vastianou Grigoriadi, Amy Hite, Ryan Dennison, Laura Hardy, Alyson Cooney, Karen Hunter, Angie Stolp, Helen Winslow, Elli Johnson, Tracie Collier, Katie Carper, Laura Beth Martin, Joycesarah McCabe, Hannah Runyan, April Hayes, Paola Barrera, Emily Lofgren, Tamara Gonzalez, Leslie Wolbert, Kelly Shank, Shelly Richardson, Heather Legge, Amanda Massingill, Jana Snyder, Andy Cockrell, Sally Olson, Tonya Papenfus, and Amy Fritz. Thank you!

And, of course, no one's voice comes from nowhere. We're all a product of voices we've heard before. We each pay attention to our own playlist of people who seem to speak personally to us, and they shape who we become. Usually they're mentors we'll never meet. Some of mine who have impacted this book include: Dorothy Sayers and her Lost Tools of Learning; Edward Deming and his 14 Points; Oswald Chambers and his passion for the sufficiency of Jesus; Ted McGrath and his story-line process; Steven Pressfield and his Muse, Resistance, and War; Shawn Coyne and his Story Grid; Tim Grahl and his ideas to help get this book in your hands; and Seth Godin and his confidence in the value of generosity.

And the voices of my family, most of whom I've never heard from back upriver—those voices that live in my heart's DNA and, I trust, are shaping me even now in ways I can never be conscious of. I hope your soul hears the voices of your upriver family too, and that you honor them by being someone who can help create the family they've always wanted.

Notes

Chapter 2 The River of Family

1. Oswald Chambers, *My Utmost for His Highest* (New York: Dodd, Mead & Company, 1935; renewed by Oswald Chambers Publications Association, 1963), 250.

Chapter 4 The Rocky River

1. Chambers, *My Utmost for His Highest*, 169.
2. Ibid., 13.

Chapter 7 Get Your Peace Right

1. Gal. 5:22–23; see also Prov. 17:9; 25:15; Eph. 4:2, 29; and Phil. 2:3.

Chapter 8 Accept Your Family, Your Role, and Your Limits

1. Elizabeth Gilbert, *Committed: A Skeptic Makes Peace with Marriage* (New York: Viking, 2010).
2. Andy Stanley, *Deep and Wide: Creating Churches Unchurched People Love to Attend* (Grand Rapids: Zondervan, 2012), 11.
3. C. S. Lewis, *The Weight of Glory* (New York: Simon and Schuster, 1996), 135–36.
4. Max Lucado, Twitter post, February 11, 2013, 11:00 a.m., https://twitter.com/maxlucado/status/301043026338390016.

Chapter 9 Be Patient, Curious, and Attentive

1. Chambers, *My Utmost for His Highest*, 169.
2. Peter Bregman, "Employees Can't Be Summed Up by a Personality Test," *Harvard Business Review*, August 19, 2015, https://hbr.org/2015/08/employees-cant-be-summed-up-by-a-personality-test.

Chapter 10 Be God's Access

1. Wess Stafford, *Too Small to Ignore: Why the Least of These Matters Most* (Colorado Springs: WaterBrook Press, 2007), 193.

2. Dale Carnegie, *How to Win Friends and Influence People* (New York: Simon and Schuster, 1936), 36.

3. Paul Tournier, *Guilt and Grace: A Psychological Study* (New York: Harper and Row, 1962), 98.

4. Simon Sinek, "How Great Leaders Inspire Action," Ted video, 18:04, filmed September 2009, https://www.ted.com/talks/simon_sinek_how_great_leaders_in spire_action.

Chapter 11 Model What You Want to See

1. "Fred Rogers Acceptance Speech—1997," YouTube video, March 26, 2008, https://www.youtube.com/watch?v=Upm9LnuCBUM.

2. *The Free Dictionary*, s.v. "perspective," http://www.thefreedictionary.com/perspective.

3. Keith Richards with James Fox, *Life* (New York: BackBay Books/Little, Brown, 2011), 47.

4. Chambers, *My Utmost for His Highest*, 250.

Chapter 12 Release Your Family, Your Role, and the Results into God's Hands

1. Andrew Murray, *With Christ in the School of Prayer* (Toronto: A. G. Watson, 1885), 99.

2. Beth Moore, *Children of the Day: 1 & 2 Thessalonians*, session 4 (Nashville: LifeWay Christian Resources, 2014), DVD.

Chapter 13 Drops of Grace into Your River

1. Chambers, *My Utmost for His Highest*, 179.

2. See William Henry Channing, *The Spirit of the Age*, vol. 1 (New York: Fowler and Wells, 1850), 408.

3. BJ Fogg, Tiny Habits, http://www.tinyhabits.com.

Chapter 14 One Big Step in Your Most Challenging Family Relationship

1. Vance Havner, *When God Breaks Through: Sermons on Revival*, comp. Dennis J. Hester (Grand Rapids: Kregal, 2003), 9.

Chapter 15 Dock of the Bay

1. Chambers, *My Utmost for His Highest*, 66.

2. C. S. Lewis, *The Four Loves: An Explanation of the Nature of Love* (New York: Harcourt, Brace, 1960), 175–76.

3. From "Dear Abby," *Times-Picayune*, New Orleans, June 17, 1981, section 3. The article that tells the story can be found at http://quoteinvestigator.com/2013/09/30/violet-forgive/#return-note-7337-17.

Acknowledgments

1. Joseph P. Lash, *Helen and Teacher: The Story of Helen Keller and Anne Sullivan Macy* (New York: Delacorte Press/Seymour Lawrence, 1980), 496.

Gary Morland is a professional communicator with a thirty-year career as a radio personality. A twenty-five-year sober alcoholic, he describes himself as "a guy who should have died but didn't, with a wife who should have left but stayed." If anyone knows the power of grace and forgiveness, it's Gary. He and his wife, Brenda, are the parents of authors Emily P. Freeman and Myquillyn Smith (The Nester). They live in North Carolina. Learn more at www .garymorland.com.

"Emily's words ignited something new and fresh and invaluable deep within me."

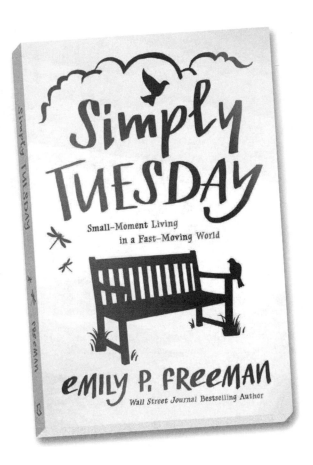

It's time to release our obsession with building a life and believe in the life Christ is building within us—one simple Tuesday at a time.

www.emilypfreeman.com

MEET **GARY MORLAND**

Follow on Facebook @GaryMorlandAuthor

Connect with Gary at **garymorland.com** to find relief in your most challenging family relationships and gain a family that roots for each other.